Reason and Argument

P. T. GEACH

Reason and Argument

OXFORD

BASIL BLACKWELL

British Library Cataloguing in Publication Data

Geach, Peter Thomas
Reason and argument
ISBN 0-631-17680-2
0-631-17280-7 Pbk.
1. Title
160   BF 455
Logic
Thought and thinking

Printed and bound by Billing and Sons Ltd
Guildford, London and Worcester

Contents

In homage to

TADEUSZ KOTARBIŃSKI

on his ninetieth birthday

Gdziekolwiek myślą sięgnąć, tkwi błędu łodyga.
Logiko, karcicielko, po badylach śmigaj!
— Na chwasty moja praca później się rozpostrze.
— A teraz czym się trudnisz?— Sama siebie ostrzę.

(from Kotarbiński's *Wesołe Smutki*)

On every side the weeds of error grow;
Vengeful logician, at them with the hoe!
'Weeding? For that just now you must not ask!'
Why not? 'Tool-sharpening is my present task.'

Preface

This is not an elementary logic book, and the name 'logic' is deliberately left out of its title; it makes no contribution to logic as a science. But logic as an everyday practice, the habit of logical thinking, is too serious a matter to be left to professional logicians: just as politics cannot safely be left to professional politicians. The notions of sound and unsound argument, of proof and logical consequence, of good grounds for thought and action, of consistency, are ones that any educated person ought to learn to handle, not just familiarly, but also with some degree of competence. Men who pride themselves on being illogical but somehow muddling through are as fatuous as men who should pride themselves on never being quite sober and trust to a Providence that looks after drunks.

The practical applications of logical thought are quite different from the development of logical theory, but not independent of it. In matters of no very great complexity, an unexpected and perhaps unwelcome consequence turns out to follow from the position one has adopted, or an unexpected inconsistency shows itself. Against such things a shrewd but untrained judgement is no safeguard. Logical thinking can be safeguarded only for minds that will submit to some elementary disciplines of formal logic. So a small amount of elementary formal logic is included in this book, though many chapters are entirely non-formal in character. I have presented the logic of terms earlier in the book than the logic of propositions, because much experience with university students convinces me that this is didactically the right order — just as in the history of logic Aristotle's formulation of term logic came before the Stoics' formulation of propositional logic. In the logic of terms it is much easier to find simple examples from ordinary discourse to which logical symbolism and methods can be directly applied; and pupils have the stimulus of success by finding exercises that they can get right with moderate effort of thought.

Many books designed to inculcate habits of logical thinking contain a little formal logic; but the formal logic they use is often the so-called traditional logic. 'Traditional' logic consists in fact of a few fragments of medieval lore (the more valuable achievements of the Schoolmen in logical theory were discarded as useless pedantic trifles) together with a large admixture of fallacy and absurdity. Since teachers of genuine logical science mostly write for their own colleagues and for university students who are reading philosophy, or again for the benefit of mathematicians, 'traditional' logicians have some success in claiming the field of ordinary discourse for their own preserve; their works sell and sell, are printed and reprinted.

The result is deplorable. A vigorous mind will find the 'traditional' logic to be a little truth in a heap of junk; under the natural though wrong impression that modern logic is meant only for mathematical intellects, such a person will decide 'Logic is not for me – I must use my mother-wit as best I can.' A less vigorous mind may be vitiated for life by bad ideas of what is logical or illogical, derived from the 'traditional' logic. The 'traditional' textbook says that it is a fallacy, the *ad hominem* fallacy, to argue against a man from *his* premises when you do not accept them yourself; that if you find no query to raise against either the premises or the form of an argument, it may be all right to reject the argument nevertheless on the score that it 'begs the question'; that a proposition may fairly be rejected in discussion if its proponent cannot meet the challenge 'Define your terms!'; that there is 'the fallacy of many questions', a logical fallacy that consists in asking whether two things both hold good *together* — the only logically correct procedure would be to divide the question into two. All of these traditional rules and warnings are logically unsound, as I hope readers of this book will learn.

In the body of the book I have not even mentioned one notorious piece of tradition, the doctrine of distributed and undistributed terms. The following two argument patterns both sin against the prohibition of undistributed middle terms, as it was traditionally understood:

Most As are Bs; most As are Cs; *ergo* some B is C

Every A is C; most Cs are Bs ⎱ *ergo* some A is B
Every B is D; most Ds are As ⎰

The reader will find, however, that methods exist for proving that both patterns are valid.

These inferences belong to the little-known field of *plurative* or *pleonotetic* logic, the logic of majorities; the eccentric but talented Edinburgh philosopher, Sir William Hamilton, must be credited with drawing attention to the obvious fact that 'most' is a quantifier, of the same category as 'all', 'some', and 'no'. The 'traditional' textbooks, one after another, say that for logical purposes 'most' is a variant form of 'some' — see e.g. A.A. Luce's *Logic* (Teach Yourself Books, E.U.P., 1975), p.54 — but this is a whopping untruth. This field is still very imperfectly explored; curious readers may learn something of the tools needed for further exploration in J.E.J. Altham's *The Logic of Plurality* (Methuen, 1971). The fragment of pleonotetic logic here presented is a *decidable* fragment, in which there is a once-for-all method of showing whether an argument form is valid or invalid. The decision method is by no means new, but its presentation in connexion with the similar decision procedures used to test syllogistic and allied arguments for validity may be something of a novelty. Here again the reader will find that he can soon master the testing techniques, and may make discoveries that surprise him even in this limited field.

In further reaches of pleonotetic logic there are even bigger surprises, of some practical importance. In political philosophy people often assume that under majority rule at least a majority of people must get what they want. But Elizabeth Anscombe recently established the following result. Suppose there is a committee of ten people, each of whom brings forward a motion: then this description of a committee-member X,

X's own motion was defeated on a simple-majority vote, and so were *most* of the motions X voted for,

may apply to an actual *majority* of members of the committee. The vague intuition that tells us this cannot happen is easily overthrown by constructing a voting-table for such a committee*. This small-scale model shows quite clearly how a democratic government may cause acute frustration to a *majority* of its citizens by a series of measures, each of which may quite truly be described as opposed only by a minority, by a 'sectional interest'; in fact, unless a good number of 'sectional interests' prevail, a country will be pretty unhappy. Consequent thinking about majorities and minorities is of obvious practical importance and is not all that easy; the aim of chapter 13 is to make some steps towards introducing disciplined reasoning about such matters.

This book grew out of a first-year course for undergraduates, most of whom were not proposing to study philosophy academically in their remaining years at the university; the aim of the course was to improve my hearers' habits of thought regardless of what their further studies might be. In the course I made constant use of an excellent

---

*I shall not reproduce Anscombe's table; the reader may try to construct one for himself.

little book *The Web of Belief*, by W.V. Quine and J.S. Ullian (New York: Random House, 1970); the reader will find several mentions of this as 'Quine and Ullian' in the text. Another very useful book of the same genre is Antony Flew's *Thinking about Thinking* (Collins Fontana, 1975). One excuse for my writing yet another such book is that I believe the discipline of thought preached by such books is attainable in practice only by using a modicum of formal logic, and consider therefore that it is useful for the reader to have this means of self-improvement within the same covers as the preaching. But indeed one needs no excuse for being a preacher of rationality; there are too few such preachers, not too many.

The University of Leeds   P.T. Geach
November 1975

1. Arguing and Giving Reasons

Philosophy as now pursued in British universities (and many others) is a highly argumentative discipline. The philosophers most studied are not sages who come out with unargued dicta, but thinkers who argue for what they think. I am not saying philosophers ought to ignore the sages; one cannot say in advance what will turn out to be philosophically interesting and important. But if we do study the dicta of some sage, we may find difficulty in accepting them; in particular, they may seem to be mutually inconsistent. The sage himself may be unwilling to engage in argument about our difficulties, and he may be right in not wanting to; but if we are to go on taking him seriously, as least his disciples ought to be ready to hear our difficulties and give reasoned answers. Even if people claim to be messengers bearing a Divine revelation, that does not dispense them from giving reasoned answers to serious enquirers. Christians in particular are enjoined to be 'ready always to give an answer to every man that asketh you a reason of the hope that is in you, with meekness and reverence' (I Peter 3.15).

Though it is reasonable to ask for reasons, it is not *always* reasonable to ask for reasons. Discussion between A and B will clearly be frustrated if B keeps on asking for a reason why he should accept what A has last said. Again, it is not reasonable to ask for a reason why one should ever observe the practice of asking for reasons; the man who claims to reject the practice must not ask others why (i.e. for what reason) they go in for it, or else he is shown not to be a total abstainer from it.

Reasons may be reasons for belief or reasons for action.

1

Human thought is both theoretical and practical: we are concerned both with the way things are and with what we ourselves have to do. In both domains there are problems to be solved, opposing considerations, and ultimate decision: and as regards both a man may be censured for hesitancy, vacillation, or pig-headed obstinacy, or again commended for wisdom in reaching decisions and firmness in adhering to what he has decided.

Here, though, a doubt may arise: is our coming to a theoretical conclusion, a conclusion as to how things are, really something for our own decision? On this matter extremely opposed views have been held; we may take Descartes and Shelley as typical supporters of the opposed views. Descartes seems to have thought belief was simply and directly a matter of choice: at least for the time being and in a time of tranquillity, you can stop believing any one of the things you now believe. Some people appear to have claimed the power to *adopt* beliefs at a moment's notice: like the White Queen who (admittedly with practice) could believe as many as six impossible things before breakfast. The Queen's words are probably an allusion to an Oxford character, W.G. ('Ideal') Ward, sometime Fellow of Balliol; he was a truculent Ultramontane in religion, and is alleged to have expressed a wish that an infallible Papal document might arrive for him to believe every morning before breakfast with *The Times*. In our own time an official of the Roman curia is similarly alleged to have said that if the Pope came out with a new decree approving artificial contraception, he himself would pass from his present certainty that this practice is wrong, to an equal certainty that it is not wrong.

This sort of command over our own beliefs is something few of us can claim; Shelley would hold it is something that nobody can truly claim. According to Shelley, if we are considering whether something is true, it is a mere matter of spontaneous feeling whether we assent or dissent or suspend judgement; feelings cannot be commanded, so neither can belief. This comes in *The Necessity of Atheism* — an interesting tract, which I regret is too inaccessible to be used as a text in the day-to-day work of philosophy departments. Shelley's grasp of the causes of human belief turned out to be very faulty; he expected his tract to stop Oxford dons from believing in the existence of God, but instead he was simply sent down.

The truth seems to lie between these two extremes. Beliefs cannot be immediately switched on or off at will; but they are to some extent under our control. We can form habits of thought which will modify our beliefs for good or ill, and the formation of such habits is certainly voluntary. It is still clearer that we can by choice hang on to threatened beliefs. Thomas Hardy has a poem about a man who manages to preserve his belief that a tombstone bearing the name of his beloved actually covers her remains, even though he could easily confirm the truth of an ugly tale he has heard — that the girl buried there is in fact a different girl and his own girl lives on as a blowzy drunken barmaid. Here, resistance to modification of belief would strike us as pitiful or contemptible; but we may regard differently the hero of Victorian romance who continues to believe in his beloved's innocence of crime, will not be moved by the damning evidence against her, and who in the dénouement when she is triumphantly vindicated can proudly say 'I always believed you were innocent even when they proved you were guilty'.

Here it is natural to bring in the threefold distinction: motives for belief, reasons for belief, causes of belief. For convenience, I am restricting 'reasons for belief' in the present context to mean: statable reasons from the truth of which it would follow, with certainty or with probability, that the belief is true. Our two lovers each had a strong motive for hanging on to the belief in the innocence of the beloved: the contrary belief if accepted would give the lover much unhappiness. But this motive affords no reason for the belief. Again, an academic exile from Ghana in the days of

'Redeemer' Nkrumah would have a strong motive for conversion to belief in Nkrumah's philosophy of Consciencism: a motive for actual belief, not only profession, because insincere profession, if detected, might make return from exile very dangerous; but here too the motive for believing affords no reason for belief.

All sorts of things may cause beliefs: a belief that black dogs are specially dangerous may be traceable to a forgotten fear in childhood, or the belief that a man is your murderous enemy may be due to brain disease. Clearly we have here neither a motive nor a reason for believing.

Sometimes a belief is adopted for motives that afford no reasons, or arises from some psychological or physiological cause again independently of any reasons, but the believer later dreams up reasons in support of the belief. This process is called *rationalization.* On the face of things, however, a grasp of reasons that would if true make out the thing believed to be certain or at least probable sometimes actually produces a belief; not all reasoning is rationalization. Some thinkers have held, or at least have been accused of holding, that *all* giving of reasons for one's own beliefs is a matter of rationalization: the stated reasons have never determined the belief arrived at, but were dreamed up after the event. If anybody really does hold this view, it is foolish of him to allege any reasons or evidence for his view; for if he is right, then other men's assent to or dissent from his view is itself something that would come about independently of their considering any reasons alleged by him. This book is written in the contrary conviction that the consideration of reasons for thinking something true *sometimes* results in the appropriate belief; if somebody does not share this conviction, he can hardly ask for reasons to be given why he should adopt it.

DISCUSSION TOPICS

1. When is it unreasonable to ask for a reason?

2. Must a good reason be a reason you could if necessary put into words? e.g.: have you a good reason, and could you put the reason into words, for believing that your parents are M. and N., or again that you have never been on the Moon?

3. How does honest giving of reasons differ from rationalization? (For this topic C.S. Lewis's *Miracles*, chapter 3, is a useful starting-point: the paperback revised version is preferable.)

2. Consistency

We wish to attain to what is true in our thinking, even though, as we have seen, there are other wishes that may form beliefs regardless of truth; and to a large extent we also wish to communicate the truth to others. Moreover, when we form plans, we wish them to be executable. To achieve these general aims, we must also aim at consistency in our thinking and talking and planning. We cannot adopt Walt Whitman's light-hearted attitude towards inconsistency:

> Do I contradict myself? Very well then, I contradict myself. I am large, I contain multitudes.

For, whether we like it or not, if we tolerate inconsistency in the thoughts we harbour and pass on to others, some of those thoughts will be false — will be at odds with the way things are in the world. Whether we like it or not, if we tolerate inconsistency in our plans, some of our plans will be frustrated. Error and frustration are no doubt our lot as men, but that is no reason for incurring them gratuitously. Consistency is not the only virtue of thinking and planning, but it is a very necessary one.

Because men are fallible, overall consistency in a man's whole corpus of beliefs is probably never achieved; and even large-scale consistency is difficult to achieve. Writers of fiction sometimes strive very hard to tell a story consistent in all its details; but in the instances when their work is rigorously tested for consistency, some failure is often apparent. Trollope actually worked with a map of his imaginary county Barsetshire; but Ronald Knox managed to show that the topographical data that can be extracted from the novels are inconsistent with the map and with one another — two sides of a triangle come out together shorter than the third side. And similar results have been reached as regards the Sherlock Holmes corpus, and even as regards some individual stories in the corpus, and have been claimed as regards George Eliot's *Middlemarch* and Tolstoy's *War and Peace*.

When it is fiction we are concerned with, these inconsistencies matter very little — if they don't offend the reader, they matter not at all. For in fiction the author is not aiming (or purporting to aim) at truth, nor yet deliberately lying; the author is only making believe to write a history of certain people and places, in order to entertain us or to teach us; and if his inconsistencies go unnoticed they will not frustrate his aim. The theory of time sketched out in Wells's *Time Machine* is grossly inconsistent; in fact the Time Traveller nimbly dances from one theory to another, and I think not one of the several theories he puts forward will on its own account stand a rigorous test for consistency; but Wells gets away with it imaginatively — only too well, for an appreciable number of philosophers are prepared to take him seriously and regard time-travel as a genuine logical possibility.

It has been said that a charge of inconsistency is an 'internal criticism' of a piece of discourse, a charge that 'does not refer to anything outside our discourse'. This view, I think, is the direct opposite of the truth. Where, as in fiction, we are not concerned to describe, or prescribe for, some reality outside discourse, inconsistency doesn't matter; it does matter in theories, historical narratives, orders, instructions, and advice, for there falsehood or practical failure is the penalty to be paid for inconsistency; so it is precisely reference to outside reality that makes inconsistency a thing to avoid if possible.

If we were always right, all our views would be consistent; as Aquinas insisted, one truth cannot conflict with another.

But we are not always right, we do not always know where
the truth lies; and we may need to assure ourselves that some
corpus of beliefs is at least consistent before being able to
find out that each member of that corpus is correct.
Logicians and mathematicians have accordingly devised
indirect proofs of consistency. It is sometimes possible to
show that one body of statements is consistent if and only if
a second body of statements is consistent; any inconsistency
that might crop up in the first set would be paralleled by a
corresponding inconsistency in the second set. Now if we
have grounds for accepting the second set as being one and all
true, the set will certainly be consistent; and accordingly the
first set of statements must likewise be consistent.

The history of non-Euclidean geometry provides an
interesting example. The Jesuit Saccheri believed that
geometry based on an axiom contrary to the Euclidean
axiom of parallels would run into inconsistency if developed
far enough; and he believed that by developing the
consequences of non-Euclidean axioms he had in fact shown
how such inconsistency arises. There were however flaws in
Saccheri's proofs, and later thinkers showed that nobody
could have succeeded where Saccheri failed. For a sort of
parallelism can be established between the deductions from
non-Euclidean axioms and the Euclidean theorems deduced
from Euclidean axioms, and in virtue of this parallelism any
inconsistency in the non-Euclidean system would be matched
by an inconsistency in the Euclidean system. Those who
believed — and Frege, for example, continued to believe —
that Euclidean geometry is actually true, and therefore
cannot be inconsistent, found themselves obliged to give up
the hope of proving the falsity of non-Euclidean geometry by
some internal inconsistency in it.

For any complicated subject-matter like this, avoidance of
inconsistency is not a matter of just avoiding a flat
inconsistency — of not asserting and then denying the same
thing. Clearly we want to avoid adopting a set of beliefs (or

indeed a set of practical policies) that are *by implication* inconsistent. But we cannot discuss the problem of what makes a position to be by implication an inconsistent position without understanding the notion of one thing's *following* from another, and learning to apply this notion in particular cases. Now what does really follow from what is not in general at all obvious to an untrained mind. When a falsehood comes out as apparently following from a truth, we know we have gone astray somewhere; but we may not easily see where — and so we may be unable to profit by the experience. And we may need to deal with a subject-matter in which we do not know when our conclusions are false and thus cannot appeal to their obvious falsity as a sign of some error in the reasoning. It would therefore be very desirable to have an art which can test our reasonings for soundness regardless of the concrete truth about the subject-matter, and can give us some assurance that if we start out with truth we shall not deviate into error. The aim of logic is to meet this need.

It is clearly self-frustrating to affirm and deny one and the same thing in the same breath, on one and the same occasion. It is not so obviously self-frustrating if we keep the assertion and the denial well apart, in different contexts of discourse: this may be called the Watertight Compartments Policy, and a good many people who seem to be reasonably efficient and happy pursue this policy. I once heard a story of a Japanese astronomer who seemed to succeed very well in treating the sun alternately as an inanimate natural body whose properties can be investigated by the techniques of mathematical physics, and as a divinity, the ancestress of the Japanese imperial dynasty; when challenged about the matter by a European colleague, he said 'Here in Europe I know it's all nonsense, but in Japan I believe it.'

In the long run the Watertight Compartments Policy cannot work. On one occasion or the other, those who follow the policy will be saying and thinking the thing that is not;

and the comforts of falsehood are short and precarious. To go in for falsehood knowingly, in the words of the prophet, is to desert the fountain of living water and hew out broken cisterns that will hold no water.

DISCUSSION TOPICS

1. Does the possibility of imagining/picturing/describing/ conceiving something show that the thing is consistently believable?

(It is helpful here to think of paradoxical pictures like M.C. Escher's.)

2. Scientists will use as working hypotheses now one, now another, of propositions not consistently combinable; does this show that they adopt the Watertight Compartments Policy, and is this policy therefore defensible after all?

3. A man says in the preface of his book that he is sure it contains errors. This statement makes the whole corpus, book *plus* preface, into an inconsistent corpus, if it was not inconsistent before. Does it follow that such self-depreciation is always logically objectionable?

3   Judgement, Belief and Knowledge: Doubt and Certainty

Belief and knowledge are states or dispositions of mind. Given that we have no reason to think there is anything wrong with his mind or brain, we unhesitatingly ascribe to a man who is presently asleep beliefs and items of knowledge that he manifested while he was awake. But besides these dispositions there are certain acts of mind which occur transiently and are traditionally called judgements: a judgement occurs at least as often as a man is confronted with a theoretical or practical problem and makes up his mind — 'This is how things are' or 'This is what I must do.' When a man makes a theoretical judgement, about the way things are, we may say of him afterwards that he knew or believed (thought) so-and-so; but it may be quite wrong to say that he still knows or believes so-and-so — the matter may have rapidly passed out of his mind without his judgement's leaving behind any dispositional knowledge or belief. If asked, as in *Hamlet*, whether a certain cloud is not very like a whale, I may judge that indeed it is; but an hour later, concerned with more important matters, I may have forgotten all about the cloud, and may no longer believe or know that the cloud I saw was like a whale. Noticing small details of one's environment and forming judgements about them is not, *pace* Sherlock Holmes, a generally useful habit. In fact, storing up such trivial knowledge permanently may be positively harmful — cf. A.R. Luria's book *The Mind of a*

11

Mnemonist; it may make one fitted only to be a gazing-stock on the stage.

Belief is sometimes favourably contrasted with unbelief; belief is a laudable disposition, unbelief a deplorable one — so we are given to understand. The contrast is spurious. Christians and Muslims used to call one another unbelievers; but the subject of the quarrel was not: which side goes in for believing, which for unbelieving? Obviously, Christians and Muslims both believed, very passionately; only they believed different dogmas. There is no more an activity or condition of unbelieving as opposed to believing than there is one of *un*seeing as opposed to seeing; belief and unbelief with respect to the same topic correspond rather to opposite ways of seeing a thing — it looks red to A, green to B, but both are seeing it.

What is opposed to a state of belief is a state of doubt, hesitancy, or uncertainty; or again a state of chosen suspense of judgement — which is a sophisticated achievement. We experience degrees of certainty and uncertainty, ranging from complete untroubled certainty to complete uncertainty.

Even the most complete certainty may turn out wrong. I may be certain that I put something in a drawer, but then look in the drawer and decide I was mistaken — and this time too certainty may be deceptive: I may be certain the thing isn't in the drawer because I've looked in the drawer and failed to see it, but the next time I look there it is, staring me in the face. These are humdrum examples: but about more important matters too we may come to doubt or deny what we previously accepted with certainty — we decide that our earlier certainty was unjustified.

Should we therefore adopt the Cartesian programme of trying to achieve a state of uncertainty, suspense of judgement, concerning all kinds of questions — or at least in all fields where by past experience we know we have been certain but wrongly so — until at the end we come to propositions that we simply cannot doubt? It is in fact psychologically impossible for a thinker to follow this programme; an attentive reader of the *Meditations* may observe many places where Descartes unhesitatingly assumes something that he would have done well to doubt, rather than doubt some of the things he in fact did doubt. Descartes was obsessed with an architectural metaphor: the house of knowledge in which we live is crumbling and unstable, so let us pull it down — living in a shack of 'provisional morality' during the process — and dig down to bedrock so as to rebuild in security. But a better metaphor for the human situation was found by the Austrian philosopher Otto Neurath: we are like sailors in a leaky ship, and we have to replace rotten timbers with sound ones while the voyage continues — we cannot get the ship into dry dock and undertake a total rebuilding of the ship.

Some philosophers have held that we can learn to be aware in our own minds of a felt difference between two kinds of certainties: one sort of felt certainty is never deceptive, it is genuine knowledge; the other sort is a mere 'taking something for granted', and this may well be mistaken. If we not only are certain, but also certain with the right kind of certainty, then we know and cannot be mistaken. Such was the teaching of certain Oxford philosophers, notably Cook Wilson and Prichard. (Prichard indeed refuses to give the name 'certainty' to that fallible state of mind which 'we may fail to distinguish' from inerrant certainty; but since he admits that this state excludes any doubt or uncertainty, it seems clearer to speak of the right and the wrong kind of certainty.)

Given the claim that is made, of ability to recognize this inerrant kind of certainty, it is fair to consider the sort of things that Prichard said he was certain of and therefore 'knew'. Prichard was certain, and therefore 'knew', that waves cannot be said, as physicists suppose, to have a velocity, since a wave is not a body and only bodies have velocities. He records, with no sense that the story might be against himself, the fact that when he said this sort of thing to physicists they thought he was 'just mad': they ought to have 'thought a bit more', but 'you cannot make a man think any more than you can make a horse drink'. (*Knowledge and Perception*, O.U.P. 1950, p.99). Furthermore, he 'knew' that his ego was a substance, and that no substance can be generated or destroyed — so that he was in the world in the days of Julius Caesar. These claims he no doubt made *bona fide* and with a feeling of certainty; but for others they may throw some doubt on Prichard's claim that he could always tell when he had the kind of certainty that cannot be wrong. Again, some other philosophers (including myself) would claim to be certain that no mere man exists at all before his mother conceives him, and that Prichard was not conceived, and therefore did not exist, till many years after the days of Julius Caesar. Prichard could of course reply that our certainty is the wrong, fallible, sort of certainty; but how is anyone to decide?

In fact, nobody who thinks consequently can get any joy out of this doctrine that there is a discernible experience of certainty that never misleads. Mr A may be certain that his certainty about some matter is the right kind of certainty; but is this second-order certainty itself a certainty of the right kind? More important, if you really are certain — whether your certainty is in fact 'knowing' or mere 'taking for granted' — then you will not be wishing to inspect your state of certainty, in order to judge whether or not it is the right kind of certainty; as soon as you do wish to undertake such an inner scrutiny, you are already in doubt, and the certainty you wished to scrutinize has vanished. In fact, when we say 'I *know*' or 'I'm *certain*', this is often a desperate attempt at self-reassurance when we are not certain and do not know. A man who is certain does not stop to scrutinize his own certainty, he just acts upon it; and then sometimes he is wrong — but it is poor consolation for that if he is told after the event by an Oxford philosopher of this school 'You see, you didn't *know*, you just took it for granted.'

Let us consider how all this applies to one particular case — memory. Memories very often come to us without any uncertainty about them; but some such memories deceive us. A man whose memory was as fallible as most of ours are and who yet decided always to trust it would have to believe that very peculiar things happened in the world, like objects disappearing from locked drawers. In fact he could scarcely avoid self-contradiction. For he would most likely resemble me in this respect: I sometimes remember the same incident in different and incompatible ways when I try to recall it on different occasions. On one or other occasion, then, memory must have been deceptive, however little doubt I felt at the time. Of course it is my present memory that tells me now how I did remember one and the same incident when I recalled it on different occasions; but I need not rely on my present memory to make my point, for if my present memory is wrong then again memory can be undoubted at the time but nevertheless wrong. And in other spheres than memory of one's own past, certainty does not exclude error.

Should this drive us to a bewildered uncertainty about everything? We certainly shall not be so driven, even if we 'logically' ought to be. Nature, as Hume remarked, has put this out of our power. A man can hold his breath for a while, but he cannot commit physical suicide by holding his breath till he dies; a man can suspend judgement in particular cases, but he cannot commit intellectual suicide by a general and persistent suspense of judgement. So we shall go on judging this or that to be certainly the case, and sometimes we shall be wrong; and there is no remedy for this either in learning to pick out the right kind of certainties or in suspense of judgement. A lot of the time, of course, we shall both be certain (so that we don't worry) and be right (so that there was nothing to worry about). And though men often err, they can correct errors, and can acquire mental discipline that makes error less frequent.

DISCUSSION TOPICS

1. When is it reasonable to apply the lawyers' maxim *'Falsus in uno falsus in omnibus'* — 'A witness who has once lied may have lied all along the line'? Does this apply to the 'testimony' of our senses or our memory, as Descartes argued?

2. Are there absolutely unshakable certainties?

3. What sorts of judgements made with certainty at the time are less liable to revision than others?

4. How much does corroboration by other people matter as regards things you yourself are certain about?

5. How is it that we are all certain that Prichard was not alive *in the body* 2,000 years ago? There are records of Mesopotamian kings, and there is the legend of the Wandering Jew, which would imply bodily life of 2,000 years; how do we know that this does not happen?

4. Inference

Arguments are always quite different from statements; this is recognised in the familiar saying 'I'm not arguing, I'm telling you!' In presenting an argument, we present certain reasons, set forth in sentences, for deriving a stated conclusion; the verbal formulations of the reasons are called the *premises* of the argument, and the transition from premises to conclusion is expressed by such words as 'and so', 'hence', 'therefore', 'consequently', 'it follows that', or (in logic books) the Latin word *'ergo'*. There is a curious tendency to confuse an argument 'So-and-so, therefore such-and-such' with a hypothetical or conditional statement employing the same sentences, 'If so-and-so, then such-and-such'. But it is easy to find examples to show the difference: 'War has been declared, so there will be a panic on the Stock Exchange' is not at all the same as 'If war has been declared, there will be a panic on the Stock Exchange'. A hypothetical statement is no more an argument than any other statement is.

In this chapter we shall consider only one use of arguments: the attainment of further truths from premises that you, the reasoner, already accept as true. You may be trying to discover truths on your own account; or on the other hand you may be trying to bring home some truth to somebody else, starting from premises that both you and he accept as true. You cannot fairly claim that your argument ought to convince the other fellow unless you and he are agreed on some stock of premises; and there certainly will be the possibility of agreement on premises, for without some accordance in your judgements you and the other could not speak and understand the same language. Of course he may make a show of challenging *any* premise you put up: like Toddy Beamish in H.G. Wells's short story *The Man who could work Miracles*, who met every attempt to get him to accept a premise with an irritating 'So *you* say!' But this cannot be anything but a ploy.

Statements are true or false; to refuse to accept a statement is to assert or suggest that the statement is false. Arguments are not statements, and cannot themselves be true or false; but the premises of an argument may be called in question as false or as not known to be true. That is one way of challenging an argument; another way is to deny or doubt the soundness of the inference from premises to conclusion — 'That's not a good reason', 'I don't see that follows'. These are the *only* two possible ways of casting doubt upon an argument: to challenge the assertion of the premises, or to dispute whether the conclusion follows from them. Sometimes people try to object to an argument on a third ground: that the conclusion is 'already implicit in' the premise, so that one who asserts the premises and then derives the conclusion is only 'begging the question'. Bad logic books list 'begging the question' as a fallacy. This objection, however, is a mere confusion, and in the court of logic it should be denied a hearing: if the conclusion really is implicit in the premises, then the argument is logically as good as can be — the conclusion really and indefeasibly follows from the premises.

A defender of the idea that begging the question is a real fault in arguments might here say: 'A question-begging argument need not be open to *logical* objection; but it is necessarily useless. If a conclusion is really implicit in the premises, surely somebody who knows the premises must already know the conclusion; so the conclusion tells him nothing new.' This protest forgets that a man may know each premise, but never happen to think of the two premises together and draw the obvious conclusion. Moreover, even with the premises before them, people vary very much in their natural or acquired ability to derive conclusions from them; having the premises is no guarantee that they will know how to derive the right conclusion. So a conclusion's being implicit in premises nowise shows that actually deriving it is a useless procedure. In C.S. Lewis's *Pilgrim's Regress*, the lady who is a personification of logic replies to the pilgrim's urgent questioning with 'I cannot tell you what I know, I can only tell you what you know.' But until logic tells him, the pilgrim may not know what *are* the things he knows.

Not all sound reasons for a conclusion are formulable as premises in which the conclusion is implicit and from which the conclusion strictly follows; we may have a good reason that is not conclusive. For instance, if our information about an individual X is simply that X belongs to a class of whose members more than 90 per cent have a certain property, then it is reasonable to conclude that X has this property: after all, this pattern of reasoning must lead from truth to truth in more than 90 per cent of the possible arguments from such pairs of true premises. But such a conclusion is defeasible by further information about X; we may even have arguments that lead opposite ways, for example:

90 per cent of Swedes are non-Catholics	90 per cent of Lourdes pilgrims are Catholics
Petersen is a Swede	Petersen is a Lourdes pilgrim
Ergo Petersen is not a Catholic	*Ergo* Petersen is a Catholic

If the premises are true, ought we to conclude that Petersen is a Catholic or that he is not?

No such difficulties arise for arguments whose conclusions follow from the premises by logical implication: what logically follows from true premises is true, and no added information can give us reason to go back on our conclusion unless it obliges us to revise our premises. When premises are supposed to give a decisive logical ground for accepting the conclusion, the argument is said to be *valid* if the conclusion really does logically follow, otherwise *invalid*.

A validly drawn conclusion spells out what is logically implicit in the premises; so valid reasoning can never lead from true premises to a false conclusion. If a conclusion does turn out false, we know that either there is falsehood in the premises, or the argument was invalid so that the conclusion did not really follow; but we may not easily see which way the argument has gone wrong. If we know that the premises are true, the fault must lie in the form of argument employed; if we know the form of argument is sound, then one or other premise must be false; but we may be unable to say definitely what is wrong with a given argument.

On the other hand, false premises, or an invalid move in argument, or both together, need not prevent our reaching a true conclusion. For example, the premise:

Everybody in Lyddon Hall speaks some language

does not yield the conclusion:

There is a language that everybody in Lyddon Hall speaks

but as it happens both are true, since everybody in Lyddon Hall speaks English. We may show that the inference is invalid by substituting for 'Lyddon Hall' the name of some organization in which everybody speaks *some* language but no language is common to all, say 'the United Nations'; in that case there would be an argument obviously 'on all fours' (as we say) with the original argument, so that one is valid if and only if the other is; but this second argument could not be valid, having a true premise and a false conclusion. Again, these two arguments are obviously 'on all fours' with one another, and both are valid arguments with a true conclusion:

All girls are mammals	All girls are serpents
All mammals are warm-blooded	All serpents are warm-blooded
Ergo All girls are warm-blooded	*Ergo* All girls are warm-blooded

but one has true premises, the other false premises.

Accordingly, if a conclusion turns out to have been supported by false premises or invalid arguments, that does nothing whatever to show the conclusion is false. To question the premises or deny the validity of some particular argument for the existence of God does not at all amount to denying or doubting the existence of God; to deny the validity of a well-known argument for the Earth's being round does not make one a Flat-Earther (a suspicion that I have myself incurred on this account).

Again, one may have good grounds for suspecting a man's testimony if he would very much wish that some state of affairs should exist, so that he may deceive himself by wishful thinking — or again, if it is very much to his interest to get people to believe his testimony, regardless of whether it is true. But no such considerations ought to affect our weighing of the arguments a man offers; knowledge of his bias or self-interest may disincline us to accept his premises on his word, but whether a conclusion follows from a set of premises can and should be judged apart from any opinions we have about the mental processes and motives of the person who employs the premises.

The conclusion of one argument may serve as a premise in a second argument, and the conclusion of that as premise in a third argument, and so on; we thus get what are called *chains* of argument or reasoning. Chains of reasoning can be very long. A chain is only as strong as its weakest link; but a logical chain, unlike a physical one, cannot break because it is too long. How are we to check over a long chain of reasoning? Descartes urged expanding by practice your ability to take in more and more steps in one apprehension. I fear this is only a way of persuading yourself that you were right, not a way of avoiding errors. Memory is indeed, as Descartes argued, perishable: but this suggests the real check — write your argument down, and get kind friends to check it as well.

DISCUSSION TOPICS

1. If landed in a foreign country without a dictionary, how could a man come to understand the language? Does agreement on the facts play an essential part in the communication between him and the native speakers? Give examples of facts on which he and they might need to agree.

2. Can there be alternative conceptual frameworks, as between which there can be *no* agreement on a set of accepted premises? If so, could a man with one such framework ever come to understand a man with another?

3. How can we know, regardless of the facts of the case, that an argument is at least not going to lead us from true premises to a false conclusion?

4. 'I am a bad reasoner, but then I know I am a bad reasoner, and this gives me an advantage; when I hear an argument I cannot refute against my cherished convictions, I simply conclude that I have been deceived by a plausible fallacy.' When *is* it reasonable to decide that an argument must be fallacious, rather than that a belief hitherto held firmly must be wrong because a valid argument disproves it?

5. Starting Points: Observation, Memory, Testimony

Much of our rational belief about the world is an inference from premises; but if we are to believe anything at all, there must be uninferred beliefs to start with. This doesn't mean that the uninferred beliefs are certain or exempt from revision. Nor need the starting points be the same for all: A and B may share a belief, but A may have to come to it by inference whereas for B it is immediate and uninferred.

It is fairly clear that observation and memory contrast with inference. The expression of judgement that a man comes up with when he observes something only counts as an observation statement if he doesn't need to make an inference but comes up with it straightaway. (This will be different for trained and untrained observers; cf. Quine and Ullian, p.19). And if I believe something about my past life because somebody else has told me or because I work it out that that's what *must* have happened, then I'm not remembering the past event in my life.

Of course a man's own memory and observation would not take him very far; he begins as a child by trusting other people's testimony without any checking or any inference, and it would be impossible for a sophisticated adult to do much checking. There are indeed ways of finding out that an authority previously trusted is unreliable; but even here each man has to rely very largely on checks performed by other people, of which he himself knows by testimony.

Obviously not all testimony is reliable; a prudent man will have learned to apply certain principles about what makes someone a poor observer or an inaccurate or untruthful reporter. These principles would be said to be 'learned from experience'. But once again it is not the prudent man's personal experience alone that teaches him these principles; he relies on the general experience of mankind about the reliability of testimony — but what the general experience of mankind amounts to is again something that he can learn only by relying on testimony.

We can rely on observation, memory, and testimony only in a general way; to attempt to accept each detail as true would land us in positive inconsistency. Must we then say: 'A man has to judge for himself'? In one way this is a triviality; in another way of taking it, plainly silly. If it means that whatever a man judges to be so, *he* is judging to be so, then this is a tautology from which nothing interesting follows; if on the other hand it means that a man is logically debarred from accepting anybody's authority about anything, then it is a plainly silly principle. A man who decides to rely on an authority is indeed making a judgement about that authority; but in so doing he is not assuming the position of a judge, not setting himself up as a higher authority. In recommending someone as a good lawyer or doctor, I am *not* claiming to be myself an even better lawyer or doctor.

DISCUSSION TOPICS

1. A judgement about what happened in the past is disqualified for being my memory if it is based on *reasons*. Can 'memory' be disqualified for the name because of the wrong *causes*? — e.g. if it is proved that a witness in court 'remembered' things because his wife had been telling him on the way to court?

2. How do we *rationally* decide that A is more reliable on a subject than B if our own independent opinion on the subject isn't worth a row of beans?

3. We commonly speak of observing somebody's pain, anger, suspicion, intention, etc. even when he doesn't verbally express them; can the corresponding statements count as observation statements? (Quine & Ullian, p.20)

6. Uses of Argument

Drawing conclusions from accepted premises in order to reach conclusions that you can accept and propound for acceptance is only one use of inference. Other uses of valid arguments are the following:

(1) Working out the consequences of imaginary cases, e.g. in school arithmetic or algebra problems or in puzzle books or in composing fiction. This use of argument is very familiar to us, but allegedly some men of primitive cultures find it very hard to grasp; and of course we had to *learn* it ourselves. Littlewood, the Cambridge mathematician, tells a story of a schoolmaster who began stating a problem: 'Suppose y is the number of eggs —' 'But Sir, please Sir, suppose y isn't the number of eggs?' (Why is this question absurd?)

(2) Testing the consequence of a supposition when you haven't yet committed yourself either way. If by validly drawing conclusions you arrive at a false result (e.g. one flatly contrary to observation) then if you are certain of all the other premises employed you know the supposition under test is false. If on the other hand you never come across a false conclusion the supposition under test is thus far confirmed. (This is called the hypothetico-deductive method: it is of use even in pure mathematics.)

(3) *Ad hominem* arguments. This Latin term indicates that these are arguments addressed to a particular man — in fact, the other fellow you are disputing with. You start from something *he* believes as a premise, and infer a conclusion he won't admit to be true. If you have not been cheating in your reasoning, you will have shown that your opponent's present

26

body of beliefs is inconsistent and it's up to him to modify it somewhere. — This argumentative trick is so unwelcome to the victim that he is likely to regard it as cheating; bad old logic books even speak of the *ad hominem* fallacy. But an *ad hominem* argument may be perfectly fair play.

Let us consider a kind of dispute that might easily arise:

A. Foxhunting ought to be abolished; it is cruel to the victim and degrading to the participants.

B. But you eat meat; and I'll bet you've never worried about whether the killing of the animals you eat is cruel to them and degrading to the butchers.

No umpire is entitled at this point to call out '*Ad hominem*! foul!' It is true that B's remark does nothing to settle the substantive question whether foxhunting should be abolished; but then B was not pretending to do this; B was challengingly asking how A could *consistently* condemn foxhunting, without also condemning something A clearly does not wish to condemn. Perhaps A could meet the challenge, perhaps not; anyhow the challenge is a fair one — as we saw, you cannot just brush aside a challenge to your consistency, or say inconsistency doesn't matter.

Ad hominem arguments are not just a way of winning a dispute: a logically sound *ad hominem* argument does a service, even if an unwelcome one, to its victim — it shows him that his present position is untenable and must be modified. Of course people often do not like to be disturbed in their comfortable inconsistencies; that is why *ad hominem* arguments have a bad name.

(4) *Reductio ad absurdum.* If a reasoner employs some premise or premises that he has only assumed for the sake of argument, then in general he is not committed to asserting the conclusion that he draws from these; like Alice who protested 'I only said "If" ', he may say 'I only said "Suppose" ' — if he didn't *assert* his premises, he is not bound to assert his conclusion and not entitled to say he has given a proof of it. But there is one important exception.

Consider a man who asserts premises P and Q and now adds a third premise R just as a supposition. If from the premises P, Q, and R all together the falsehood of R logically follows, then the reasoner's assertion of P and Q warrants him in going on to *assert* that R is false, and in offering this as a *proved* conclusion to anyone who agrees in accepting P and Q. For if R could be asserted along with P and Q, the set of asserted premises P, Q, R would logically lead to the assertion both of R and of R's falsehood, and this is absurd. This powerful argumentative move is called *reductio ad absurdum*.

We must carefully notice that in drawing a conclusion by *reductio ad absurdum* the reasoner is not revoking a false move of assuming R; he never did *assert* R, and to assume a premise for the sake of argument is in no case a mistake. Of course it is possible for a man to begin by *asserting* P, Q, and R and then discover that the falsehood of R follows; in this case he *has* made a mistake, and must put it right by going back on the assertion of one or other premise; he cannot acquiesce in self-contradiction.

An example from the topic of testimony which we were considering just now may serve to show the difference between a sound *reductio ad absurdum* procedure and a lapse into muddle and self-contradiction. Many of us have heard the story of psychological experiments to show how inaccurately eye-witnesses will report a series of incidents. So far as I am concerned these stories are mere hearsay; I have never met anyone who claimed to have been present on such an occasion. But suppose I had met such a person, M.N. Then I could reason as follows:

M.N. claims to have witnessed such-and-such psychological experiments.
Let us suppose that eye-witness testimony is never seriously unreliable.
Then such-and-such experiments had the results that M.N. reports.

But if the results were such as M.N. reports, some eye-witness testimony is seriously unreliable (because the eye-witness testimony of the people used as subjects of the experiment will have turned out to be so).
So, some eye-witness testimony *is* seriously unreliable.

This argument is a sound *reductio ad absurdum*, and would warrant one in asserting its conclusion. Notice that in drawing the conclusion I do not *assert* the premise that eye-witness testimony is reliable in order to draw the conclusion that it is not; what I *assert* about M.N. is not that he reliably gave such-and-such testimony, but only that he gave it — and if he was inaccurate or mendacious in giving it, then so far from throwing doubt on my conclusion this confirms it.

On the other hand, people often appear prepared to believe without question the accounts given of such experimental results, and to say that here there is 'scientific proof' that eye-witness testimony, e.g. in law-courts, is unreliable. It is very difficult to make sense of such a position. Probably those who maintain it will be going by hearsay, which on any view is less reliable than eye-witness testimony; but even in the most favourable case, that they have heard or read an eye-witness of the experiments, they are indefensibly inconsistent. For in order to be warranted in asserting that the experiments happened as described, they have to *assert* the reliability of *this* eye-witness; but the ultimate conclusion casts doubt on the testimony of eye-witnesses; and then what makes the position different for the eye-witness of these experiments? The mere fact of his evidence, as we have seen, affords a valid *reductio ad absurdum* proof that eye-witness testimonies may be very unreliable; but then just on that account we can and should be chary of believing all the tales emanating from psychology labs. (*Some* such tales — like the tale I once heard of a young ape that could talk just like a young human child — bear the stamp of fraud or self-deception upon their face.)

Reduction ad absurdum is a tool for obtaining knowledge, not just a good dialectical trick. G.H. Hardy the Cambridge mathematician said that *reductio ad absurdum* is a much more brilliant move than any chess sacrifice; in order to win the game, you offer, not some major piece, but *the game*. An example of a particularly brilliant move comes in Euclid. Euclid attacks the problem whether the prime numbers — which become rarer and rarer as we go on in the number series — finally peter out altogether: whether there is a biggest prime number, beyond which there are no more prime numbers. He proves that there is no biggest prime number by assuming that there is one! Suppose P is the biggest prime number. Then multiply together all the prime numbers up to and including P, and add 1. The resulting number, N say, clearly has not as a prime factor any of the prime numbers up to P; for there will upon division always be a remainder 1 (1 itself does not count as a prime number). So this number N will have some prime factor bigger than P; N may of course be prime itself, but then N is obviously bigger than P, so it makes no difference if N is its own only prime factor. So P is *not* the biggest prime number. We have reached this result by *assuming* (not asserting) that P *is* the biggest prime number, and using along the way some obvious truths about numbers, which we asserted; we are now entitled to *assert* that P is *not* the biggest prime number, regardless of which number P may be — i.e. that there is no biggest prime number.

DISCUSSION TOPICS

1. What is the difference between validly deriving a conclusion and proving it?

2. Aristotle said that the rules for deriving conclusions were just the same for demonstrative reasoning (from premises you are taking to be known) and for dialectical reasoning (from premises you just assume for argument's sake). Was Aristotle right?

3. If you reason *ad hominem* from a premise which your opponent believes true, but you know to be false, why isn't this cheating? Why is it any better than using a method of argument which you know is unsound but your opponent can be got to take as sound?

4. '*Reductio ad absurdum* is a ridiculous procedure. You claim to have proved a conclusion; but if you have proved it, then on your own showing one of the premises you've used is false; and how can you *prove* anything from use of a false premise? Deductions from false premises are as likely to be false as to be true.' Does this show the method is unsound?

7. Logical Validity

If starting from truth we are led into falsehood, we know our conclusion has been drawn by an invalid process. Contrariwise, it is sometimes obvious in a particular instance that a conclusion follows from premises — we need not know whether conclusion and premises were true or not.

We can satisfy ourselves that a conclusion follows from premises, when this is not obvious, by constructing a chain from premises to conclusion of little links, every one obvious. 'One step enough for me'!

In a rough and ready way we can test an argument for validity/invalidity, when in doubt, by observing that it is 'on all fours with' an argument patently invalid. 'You might as well say. . .' But this is a very hit-or-miss procedure. The only method we can rely on is to devise a way of showing the logical form common to arguments that are 'on all fours with' each other. This was Aristotle's achievement; nobody, as far as we know, had thought of such a thing before; we still use his term 'schema' (plural 'schemata') for the way of setting out an abstract logical pattern. Logical schemata are the very backbone of logic: we shall come to discuss them in Chapter 10. Before getting on to logical schemata, we need a clear idea of *propositions* and *contradictories*.

As we saw in the last chapter, when an argument is put forward by someone who claims to conclusion follows, that person is not *necessarily* vouching for the truth of either premises or conclusion. So we should say that logical rules of inference are concerned with *propositions*, theses put forward for consideration, not necessarily with statements i.e. *asserted* propositions. A proposition is true or false regardless of whether you assert it. When you vouch for a conclusion's following, you do not vouch for its truth unless you have committed yourself to asserting the premises.

Any proposition can be regarded as one of the two possible answers to a yes-or-no question. The *contradictory* of a proposition is the other one of the two possible answers. It is often not obvious whether two propositions *are* contradictories. You can mechanically form a contradictory by sticking 'It is not the case that' in front of a proposition. Another word for the contradictory of a proposition is: the *negation* of a proposition. Since negation means switching from *yes* to *no*, or from *no* to *yes*, as an answer to a certain question, double negation cancels out, and gets us back to the answer we started with.

EXERCISES

1. See if you can construct an argument on all fours with the plausible but invalid argument
   Everything is caused by something else: *ergo* something causes everything else.
(The argument constructed should be patently invalid.)

2. Is the following argument valid or invalid? How would you settle the matter?
   Most Swedes are Protestants; most Swedes who visit Lourdes are not Protestants;
   ergo Most Swedes do not visit Lourdes.

3. Are these pairs of propositions contradictories? Are they the *yes* and the *no* answers to the same questions?
   If B is to survive, he must drink the water from his

water-bottle.
If B is to survive, he must not drink the water from his water-bottle.
(Can you imagine poor old B in a predicament that makes both these things true?)

The Museum is open till October.
The Museum is not open till October.

The phrase 'is not' is in this sentence.
The phrase 'is not' is not in this sentence.

8. Truth and Falsehood

We have kept on using the word 'true' without explanation or definition; this does not mean that we had no right to use the word, nor yet that we understand the word so well that no problems can arise about it.

'True' is variously applied; we shall be concerned with the use of 'true' — or as the case may be 'false' — to characterize what people say. What people say is true or false whether they are *asserting* it or not: if I say 'It is false to hold that the Earth is flat', the sub-sentence 'the Earth is flat' is false; and that is why what I myself do assert — 'It is false to hold *that*' — is true. Nobody need have actually asserted that the Earth is flat — even though in fact some people have done so — to make what *I* say true.

'Contradictory' or 'negation' being explained as in chapter 7, a proposition is false if and only if its negation or contradictory is true, and true if and only if its negation or contradictory is false. So, of any two contradictories, one is true and one false — unless it can be said that the yes-no question to which both are answers is a question that 'does not arise'. (Just when this *can* properly be said is a point much disputed among philosophers; I cannot enter into the dispute here.)

Some philosophers think there are different brands of truth — empirical or factual truth, logical truth, mathematical truth, religious truth, etc. But such principles as that a falsehood cannot be inferred from a set of truths take no account of these supposed differences in brand of truth.

If we take any specific proposition, we see that ascribing truth to it hardly ever raises any problem about truth — still

35

less about the alleged kinds of truth or senses of 'true'. If the proposition comes to us in a foreign tongue or unfamiliar jargon, then indeed we do not know what ascribing truth to it amounts to; but once this obstacle is overcome, the problem of truth as such vanishes. Let A be the proposition 'Our liege Lord and Sovereign is deceased'; once we know that A just means 'Our King is dead', ascribing truth to A raises all and only the problems of ascribing death to the King. Death is indeed a philosophical problem − but the truth of death-notices is not an extra problem.

Further reason for scouting the idea of brands of truth or senses of 'true' may be apparent if we consider the figure of speech called asseveration. We say 'So-and-so as sure as such-and-such' − we affirm the first-uttered proposition very strongly by thus linking it to the allegedly obvious truth of the second. 'He's guilty, as sure as I'm standing here; he'll soon be caught, as sure as eggs are eggs; and then he'll swing, as sure as God made little apples.' The effectiveness of the asseverations depends only on whether the propositions put forward after 'as sure as' are acceptable as obvious truths: no matter that one truth would be observational, a second logical, and the last religious.

Logicians recently introduced the term 'the truth-value of a proposition' to mean its truth if it is true and its falsehood if it is false. They also speak of truth-conditions, meaning necessary and sufficient conditions for a proposition's being true: e.g. a conjunction, an 'and' proposition, is true if and only if each conjoined proposition is true. The word 'iff' is short for 'if and only if'.

DISCUSSION TOPICS

1. Does 'It is true that Smith drinks too much' mean the

same as 'Smith drinks too much?' And does 'It is false that the Earth is flat' mean the same as 'The Earth is not flat'?

2. Can a criterion of truth be given e.g. 'A statement is true iff it is useful to believe it', or 'iff it fits into a coherent system of statements'?

3. Are logicians justified in abstracting from the *kind* of truth concerned and stating principles like 'From truths only truths can be inferred'?

9. Definition

In a work like the present the topic of definition can be only briefly, and therefore inadequately, discussed. One valuable aid to further thought on the subject is Richard Robinson's book *Definition* (O.U.P., 1972) — a book of much wit and insight, adorned with a rich variety of well-selected examples, both of definitions themselves and of rules and theories formulated for definition.

In non-academic debates, by word of mouth or in the columns of newspapers, 'Define your terms!' is a frequent move: 'Let us first of all agree on the definition of our terms' is more polite and less peremptory, but not logically a different move. But clearly this is not a demand that can always legitimately be made. If a definition is given in words, the demand might again be made that *these* words be defined — and there would be no end to it, or rather the discussion could never begin, never get under way. 'Define your terms!' is as effective a discussion-stopper as Toddy Beamish's way of meeting every premise put up for his assent with 'So *you* say!' It is just as unreasonable, too; for of course our ability to understand our fellow-men, and our right to assent to what they say, cannot depend on the production of formal definitions in words for the terms employed. Of course our mutual understanding is very often imperfect; but then producing a formal definition in words is not necessarily either the only way or the best way of removing the misunderstanding.

Socrates used to maintain that nobody has the right to maintain a thesis unless he is prepared (if challenged) to produce a definition of the key words used in stating the thesis: inability to do this means that you didn't know what you were talking about in stating the thesis. It would really have served him right if one of his victims had retorted: 'Come now, Socrates, please define "definition"!' and given him a taste of his own medicine; 'So you can't define "definition" satisfactorily? Very well then: *you* don't know what *you* are talking about when you say we must be able to give definitions — so I need pay no further attention to your time-wasting dialectic.' In concrete instances, the Socratic demand is preposterous. I certainly could not define either 'oak-tree' or 'elephant'; but this does not destroy my right to assert that no oak-tree is an elephant, nor will my readers find this thesis hard to understand or be likely to challenge it.

Socrates demanded not merely a definition, but one that would enable one to decide marginal and doubtful cases. This demand is still more unreasonable. To return to my example: there might well be animals and plants around about which I should be quite unable to decide whether they are elephants, or whether they are oak-trees, as the case may be; but anything that is even marginally likely to count as an oak is certainly no elephant, and anything that is even marginally likely to count as an elephant is certainly no oak-tree.

Socratic dialectic was believed at the time to be morally pernicious. One can indeed well imagine that a man might be morally harmed if he decided he must suspend judgement as to whether swindling is unjust until he has watertight definitions of 'swindling' and 'unjust'. In moral philosophy of our time there are to be found arguments in the Socratic style. The following fairly shows the sort of thing we get. 'What is life? Can we define the moment of death? Can we, moreover, define the difference between actually killing and just failing to preserve life? And what is a baby? Would fine healthy puppy-dogs brought forth by a human mother count as babies? — If you can't answer these questions, you have no right to say with any confidence that it's wrong to kill babies, since you don't know what you mean by "killing" or "baby".' The demand 'Define your terms!' is not harmful only in theory.

The right reply to a moral philosopher who argues like this is not to try to answer his questions, but to remind him about oak-trees and elephants; there are clear specimens of these, even if there are also marginal cases; and similarly there are cases in which some proposed act would quite clearly be killing a baby, even if there are also marginal cases. Nor is anybody logically obliged to say how he would apply his terms in the fantastic cases dreamed up by moral philosophers, and say e.g. whether we'd be dealing with babies if a human mother brought forth puppy-dogs; he can simply reply in the style of Dickens's Tommy Traddles 'But she wouldn't, you know; so if you please we won't suppose it.'

In theory, in speculation, the Socratic view of definitions has been very harmful. One useful way of coming to understand the meaning of an imperfectly clear term is to produce some good example where the term plainly applies. Plato represents Socrates as objecting to this procedure: unless we already know quite well what the term means, there will be no unexceptionable examples to show us; so examples are useless anyhow. The truth is that if misunderstanding arises it may be resolved *either* by producing criteria for using a term *or* by giving good clear examples: we can work from examples to get criteria that will fit them, and we can use criteria to apply the term to new examples. But if we have *neither* criteria *nor* examples, the original misunderstanding may persist; in the typical Socratic enquiry, a definition is still to find, but examples are rejected — so it is no wonder that the ostensible purpose of the enquiry is foiled in the ensuing impasse, though the disputants have good clean philosophical fun on the way.

A way of explaining terms quite different from verbal definition is *ostensive* explanation or definition: pointing to a typical case of the term's correct application and saying

'That's so-and-so.' Realizing that if all terms must be defined with only verbal definitions we could never get started, philosophers have sometimes held that we ought to start with *ostensive* definitions, and then define other words directly or indirectly in terms of these. But there is a difficulty about assigning to ostensive definition this primitive and fundamental role. If the pupil already grasps what *sort* of word is being ostensively explained, e.g. that it is a name of a person, a colour-adjective, a word for a direction like 'north', etc., then ostensive teaching may enable him to fill a gap in his understanding; if he fails to grasp this, he may ludicrously misunderstand. Now which sort of word a word is, is a matter of its use in the context of a sentence; and it would be a miracle if ostensive teaching of single words conveyed this. Ostensive definition has sometimes been supposed to play a dominant role in the child's learning of its first language. But in fact it plays a very minor role: children come to understand words used in sentences, which themselves have meaning as wholes in human beings' physical environment and in connexion with practical activities; and after a time the children come to understand new combinations of words and to produce new combinations themselves. Philosophical theories of knowledge and meaning, and psychological theories of language learning, are doomed to futility if this fact is forgotten or played down.

It has long been traditional to distinguish between *real* and *nominal* definitions. Real definitions aim at marking out a class of things that shall correspond to a natural kind, like gold or acids. Locke despaired of finding natural kinds in the world, but prematurely so; the unreliable behaviour of chemicals called by a given name, which was so frustrating to chemists of Locke's day, was removed by better methods of preparing and purifying substances. Locke conceived of the kinds of things in the world as forming a continuous spectrum, in which men made arbitrary divisions for practical purposes; but in fact the spectrum itself shows the defect of this view — spectral lines correspond to the radiations of definite chemical elements, whose properties, we believe, remain the same even in remote stars whose spectra we observe. We need, then, to recognise the natural kinds of things, and to conceptualize this recognition in a form of words describing a given kind: such is the real definition, which naturally scientists keep on updating.

Nominal definition on the contrary is concerned with the use of a term. One sort of nominal definition accepts established usage, and is concerned to sort out and characterize as accurately as possible the actual uses of a word; this is the sort of definition you find in a good dictionary — though dictionaries will also contain a certain number of what would count as *real* definitions, of the sort just described. Another sort of nominal definition does not merely accept whatever happens to be current usage, but constitutes a proposal for tightening up the use of a term; under the proposal, the term would mostly be applied as it now is, but with stricter criteria; or again, the proponent of the definition may suggest that we abandon some current uses and retain only one preferred use. Finally, an old word may be arbitrarily given a quite new meaning — as when Humpty Dumpty stipulated that 'glory' shall mean 'a knock-down argument'. This is harmless so long as the new arbitrarily conferred meaning is far enough away from the old meaning; but philosophers have often unwisely introduced terms thus defined by stipulations into contexts where the reader could easily slip back unawares into the familiar old meaning; and I am afraid some philosophers have then deceived themselves, as well as baffling their readers.

Mathematicians have an old custom of picking up words from the market-place and giving them new meanings in Humpty-Dumpty style. Our 'sphere', 'cone', 'cylinder', 'pyramid', come from Greek; the Greek geometers used the common words for 'ball', 'pine-cone', 'garden roller', and 'wheat-cake', and of course this caused no confusion. In modern mathematical jargon we find such words as 'lattice', 'ring', 'chain', and 'filter'. But even in mathematics the risk of confusion coming about from the familiar use of words is not altogether negligible: it could be shown, I believe, that fundamentally confused intuitions in set theory arise from associating the mathematical terms 'set' and 'class' with such familiar uses as we get in 'chess set' and 'Bible class'.

A special caution is needed about the definition of *relative* terms — words expressing relationship, like 'father'. We must first explain what it is for A to be father of B; then we can explain what being a father is — 'being a father' means 'being father of *somebody*'. Who is father of whom determines who belongs to the class of fathers, not the other way round; we could not start with the idea of just being a father, and then explain being father *of* A in terms of some way that A *has* or *possesses* 'his' father. (This is the point of the old Greek sophism that if a dog is a father and is yours he is your father: why does this not follow, since a dog that is a spaniel and is yours is your spaniel?) In this case the matter is perhaps obvious enough; but many faulty definitions of terms have been given which sin against the principle here illustrated; for example, purporting to define the term 'number' rather than 'the number *of As*'. or the term 'love' rather than 'love for a person X by a person Y'.

An important class of definitions are *recursive* definitions. One might for example define 'ancestor' as follows: A is B's ancestor if and only if (either A is B's parent, or A is parent of an ancestor of B). The term to be defined recurs in the definition, but that by no means makes it useless; it is an immediate consequence that B's parents are his ancestors, and it can be shown in a few steps that B's father's mother's father's mother is an ancestor of B.

Recursive definitions are of frequent use in symbolic logic and mathematics. For example, the power notation may be explained thus, if 'n' stands for a whole number:

If $n = 0$, $a^n = 1$; if $n > 0$, $a^n = a \times a^{n-1}$

It clearly does not get us into a vicious regress that there is an instance of the power notation in the formula used to explain this notation; for given which numbers a and n are, we can work out in a finite number of steps which number a^n is — e.g. 3^5 is $3 \times 3 \times 3 \times 3 \times 3 \times 1$ or 243.

Again, recursive explanations are often used in logic to characterize the class of well-formed formulas (wffs) in some part of logic, some restricted logical calculus. For example, the wffs of the equivalential calculus, written in Polish notation, may be characterized as follows:

1. The letters 'p,q,r' — with or without primes (') attached to them — are wffs.* (Each of these letters is short for some arbitrarily chosen proposition.)
2. The letter 'E' followed by two wffs of the equivalential calculus is a wff. ('Epq' is read as 'p if and only if q'.)
3. There are no other wffs in the calculus.

Given this recursive explanation, we can work out step by step which strings of letters are wffs (and what these mean) and which are not wffs. For example, 'E'p'q', 'pqEr', 'EEpqrs', are not wffs; but 'EEpq'Eq'p' is a wff, meaning '(p if and only if q') if and only if (q' if and only if p)'.

DISCUSSION TOPICS

1. Must the object of a real definition actually exist? (Could there be a real definition of a chemical substance which does not occur naturally and has not yet been synthesized?)

2. What is the objection to circular definition? Why does this not apply to recursive definitions?

---

*In the slang of logicians, 'wff' is pronounced 'woof'.

3. We often hear that A is B 'by definition'. What does this mean? Can a definition make a proposition to be true?

4. Discuss some of the definitions offered by philosophers which may be held to sin against our canon for defining relative terms.

10. Logical Schemata

The following three arguments, though obviously different in grammatical form, are instances of a single logical form:

(1) Every philosopher is mortal; Socrates is a philosopher; therefore Socrates is mortal.

(2) Edith envies everybody luckier than Edith; Herbert is luckier than Edith; therefore Edith envies Herbert.

(3) Herbert is less lucky than everybody who envies Herbert; Edith envies Herbert; therefore Herbert is less lucky than Edith.

The only practical way of representing a logical form is the one invented by Aristotle; in this instance we should get:

(4) Every F is G; *a* is F; therefore *a* is G.

The letters 'F', 'G' and '*a*' are called *schematic letters* and (4) is called a *schema* (a term coming down from Aristotle). Textbooks often use the word 'variables'; but they use this term also for other uses of single letters — these will not concern us for the present.

Each schematic letter has a certain range of *interpretations*: the small letter '*a*' is a letter representing proper names. When we pass from '*a* to G' to 'Socrates is a man' we are interpreting '*a*' by 'Socrates'. We speak of the *category* of proper names.

It is convenient to consider in the first instance arguments concerned with objects contained within some definite class. This class is called the Universe of Discourse. The Universe for the arguments we are presently considering is the class of human beings.

There are various things that hold good or do not hold good of each object in such a Universe; e.g. that he/she *is a philosopher*, that Edith envies him/her, that he/she is *luckier than Edith*. Expressions for what holds good or does not hold good of objects in a Universe are called *predicates*. Predicates are a different category from proper names. The big letters 'F' and 'G' represent predicates.

The word 'is' is a mere concession to English idiom and plays no essential logical role (cf. Russian: 'John clever', 'John rascal'). In logic a proper name and a predicate fit together to make a sentence; logicians regularly use the notation 'Fa' rather than the 'a is F' that I have been using. So there's no objection to counting 'Edith envies Herbert' and 'Socrates is mortal' as two concrete interpretations of 'Fa', even though one has an 'is' in it and the other doesn't.

The quickest and easiest way to give interpretations of predicate letters is to stick in an asterisk, '*'; this is a mere gap-filling sign — the gap may be filled with the name of *any* old object in the Universe. Thus given:

a = Edith, F* = * envies Herbert   or again
a = Herbert, F* = Edith envies *

we get 'Edith envies Herbert' as the reading of 'Fa' or 'a is F'. (*Both* interpretations work.)

And with the readings

F* = * is luckier than Edith   G* = Edith envies *

'Every F is G' will be interpreted as 'Every(body who is) luckier than Edith, Edith envies'. The '—body' part of 'everybody' expresses the choice of Universe; and 'who is' is just a bit of English grammar — these words could be left out in another language (say Latin).

'Every', 'some', and 'no' belong neither to the category of names nor to that of predicates; they are *quantifiers*. Phrases like 'every man' and 'some man' seem more like names than predicates or quantifiers do; but jokes about 'no man' as a name are about 3000 years old, and it's not too hard to see that whereas 'Socrates' names Socrates, 'every man' doesn't name every man nor 'some man' some man.

A schema may be valid, in which case *all* its interpretations are valid. (4) is a valid schema. Any sound and conclusive argument is reducible to a valid schema. This does not mean: to one of the valid schemata discussed in chapters 10-13 of the present book. We shall later consider schemata in which the interpretations of the schematic letters belong to the category, not of predicates or of proper names, but of propositions; and there are many other schemata, bringing in expressions of yet other categories as the required interpretations. But any valid argument is reducible in principle to *some* valid schema; if our existing logic cannot supply such a schema, that only means we need to develop logic a bit further.

It may be necessary to add a truistic premise that can be taken as generally admitted: e.g. 'Every man is an animal' is a truism needed to reduce 'Socrates is a man, therefore Socrates is an animal' to schema (4). An argument purporting to be conclusive but not reducible to a valid schema is invalid. The use of schemata is to give us tests for validity other than the hit-or-miss method of finding an obviously valid or invalid argument that is sufficiently 'on all fours with' the argument under test.

We represent a conjunction of predicates just by writing predicate letters side by side. Thus if 'F*' represents '* is a philosopher' and 'G*' represents 'Murdoch dislikes *', then 'FG*' represents '* is a philosopher *and* Murdoch dislikes *'.

Every predicate, like every proposition, has a negation or contradictory: we represent this by putting a dash (') after the sign for a predicate. Thus if 'K*' represents '* admires Wittgenstein', then 'K'*' represents '* does *not* admire Wittgenstein'.

With letters read as above, and the Universe taken to be people, the categorical schema 'Every FK' is G' will come out as:

Every person who *is a philosopher* and *does not admire Wittgenstein, Murdoch dislikes.*

or: Murdoch dislikes every philosopher who does not admire Wittgenstein.

The skill of translating from schemata to English sentences, from English sentences to schemata, with the aid of a 'dictionary' that specifies the Universe of Discourse and interprets the schematic letters, is one that can be acquired only by practice: like learning a foreign language.

The following two exercises are worked out in slow motion, step by step. With practice, especially in simpler exercises, much of the work will become mental work; you will then not need to set out each step on paper.

I. To translate into English the schema 'Any AB is C''.
    Univ. = persons; A* = * is a husband, B* = * drinks heavily, C* = the wife of * will have enough housekeeping money.

    Step 1 Introduce mention of the Universe into the schema.
    Result: Any person who is AB is C'
    Step 2 Expand all conjunctions of predicate letters.
    Result: Any person who is A and (who) is B is C'
    Step 3 The *grammatical* predicate of the original schema is '* is C'' where the star marks an empty place. Interpret '* is C''.
    Result: Since 'C*' or equivalently '* is C' is to be read as:

    the wife of * will have enough housekeeping money, the contradictory '* is C'' will have to be read as:

    the wife of * will *not* have enough housekeeping money.

    Step 4 In the empty place (marked with the star) of the result of Step 3, insert the phrase used in Step 2, 'any person who is A and who is B'.

Result: The wife of any person who is A and who is B will not have enough housekeeping money.

Step 5 Use the 'dictionary' to interpret the relative clauses 'who is A' and 'who is B'.

Since '* is A' is to be read as '* is a husband', 'who is A' becomes 'who is a husband'. Since '* is B' is to be read as '* drinks heavily', 'who is B' is to be read as 'who drinks heavily'.

Result of Step 5:

The wife of any (person who is a) husband (and) who drinks heavily will not have enough housekeeping money.

II. To express in a logical schema the sentence:

The wife of any husband who drinks heavily will not have enough housekeeping money.

Univ. = persons; A* = * is a wife, B* = *'s husband drinks heavily, C* = * will have enough housekeeping money.

(Notice that this is not at all the same 'dictionary' as in Exercise I.)

Step 1 A moment's thought shows that this example does *not* contain a 'definite description' purporting to describe just *one* wife, as in the sentence:

The wife of Sir Isaac Harman was arrested,

but is about *any* wife, *any* person who is a wife and who (etc.). We may in fact paraphrase the sentence, bringing in the Universe explicitly, as follows:

Any person who is a wife and whose husband drinks heavily will not have enough housekeeping money.

Step 2 Replace the relative clauses 'who is a wife' and 'whose husband drinks heavily' by clauses containing schematic letters.

Since '* is a wife' is the rendering of 'A*' or '* is A', we rewrite 'who is a wife' as 'who is A'.

Since '*'s' husband drinks heavily' is the rendering of 'B*' or '* is B', we rewrite 'whose husband drinks heavily' as 'who is B'.

Result of Step 2:

Any person who is A and (who) is B will not have enough housekeeping money.

Step 3 Replace the remaining English predicate in the result of Step 2 by using a schematic letter in the 'dictionary'.

Result of Step 3:

Any person who is A and is B is C′:

for, in view of the dictionary entry for 'C*' or '* is C', '* is C′' will come out thus: '* will *not* have enough housekeeping money.'

Step 4 We contract 'is A and is B' to 'is AB'.

Result: Any person who is AB is C′

Step 5 We now omit mention of the Universe, which is not needed since the 'dictionary' tells us what the Universe is for interpreting the schema.

Result: Any AB is C′.

In exercises like (II), you may not be *given* a 'dictionary', but have to *invent* a 'dictionary' that will turn an English sentence into a schema.

EXERCISES

1. If we use the bogus key of interpretation (Universe = human beings): a = every Dane (or a = some Dane), F* = * is a philosopher, G* = * is mortal we seem to obtain these arguments from schema (4):

(5) Every philosopher is mortal: every Dane is a philosopher:

therefore every Dane is mortal.

(6) Every philosopher is mortal: some Dane is a philosopher:

therefore some Dane is mortal.
Are (5) and (6) valid or invalid arguments? If they are both valid, why should this method of interpretation be rejected as bogus?

2. What schemata do we get from (5) and (6) by way of the key of interpretation:
    F* = * is a philosopher, G* = * is a Dane, K* = * is mortal?

3. Represent, with the following key of interpretation (Universe = human beings; F* = * is a philosopher, G* = Murdoch dislikes *, K = * admires Wittgenstein
the following two sentences:
    Everyone who admires Wittgenstein is a philosopher
    Murdoch dislikes everyone who is not a philosopher
What is the interpretation of 'Every FG′ is K′'?

11. Existential Import of Categorical Schemata

This formidable title just means: What does a categorical proposition, schematically represented, imply as to what there is or is not to be found in the given Universe?

'No' schemata are easy; 'No F is G' means that nothing occurs in the Universe that both is F and is G. 'Some F is G' is treated as true if *at least one* thing both is F and is G, and implies no more than this. In ordinary language 'some' may be double-edged: 'Some men are wise' may be meant to imply '. . . and others are otherwise'. But if such an implication is intended in formal logic, it must be made explicit: 'Some F is G *and* some F is G''.

About 'every' forms there are differing conventions. In ordinary language there are proverbial expressions where the very point is *not* to infer 'Some F is G' from 'Every F is G':

(1) Every rainbow's end has a crock of gold buried under it.

(2) Every honest miller has a golden thumb.

There is here implied a reading of 'Every F is G' as meaning simply 'No F is G''.

(1) Univ. = places on Earth; F* = * is the end of a rainbow;

   G* = a crock of gold is buried under *

(2) Univ = persons: F* = * is an honest miller; G* = * has a golden thumb.

And it is further hinted (though not logically implied) that 'No F is G'' comes out true because nothing in the Universe is F. On the other hand, many ordinary-language 'every' propositions clearly are meant to imply the corresponding 'some' propositions: e.g. 'Everybody in this room perfectly understands logic'. (A logical example need not be true. False propositions can figure as premises and conclusions in logical work; in fact it is by drawing conclusions from a false proposition that we find out it *is* false.)

Some logic texts (Lewis Carroll in *Symbolic Logic* and *The Game of Logic*) use this convention — that 'Every F is G' does imply 'Some F is G'. In that case the rainbow's end and honest miller examples will *not* be represented as 'Every F is G' *but* as 'No F is G'', whereas the example about people in this room will be represented by 'Every F is G'. (Work out a specification of the Universe and interpretation of 'F*' and 'G*' for this last example.)

Most recent texts follow a different convention — that 'Every F is G' is always equivalent to 'No F is G'' and no more. In that case the example about people in this room will be represented *not* by 'Every F is G' but by 'Every F is G *and* some F is G'.

This is a matter of convention, purely. In working examples follow this practice:

(1) As regards an ordinary-language 'every' proposition, consider whether it is the *likely* meaning that the 'some' proposition is also implied; settle this before you pass from English to schemata.
(2) State which convention you are employing for the 'every' form in schemata, and stick to that convention.

Any one of the categorical forms can be reduced to an existential proposition to the effect that in the Universe there are or are not things answering to some complex description. Thus if we write '= 0' to show that there are *no* things in the Universe answering a given description, and '≠ 0' to show that there are *some* such things, we get the following results:

Some F is G	$FG \neq 0$
No F is G	$FG = 0$
Every F is G	$FG' = 0$
	(or with Lewis Carroll's convention:
	$FG' = 0$ *and* $FG \neq 0$).

DISCUSSION TOPIC

In the existential way of reading categoricals, a 'no' proposition comes out to the effect that a certain complex description, formed out of predicates that apply in a given Universe, describes nothing in that Universe. Is there anything wrong with the idea of a description that describes nothing? Must such a description be self-contradictory?

(What is the point of writing — as a chemist in fact did — a chemical treatise on *Nonexistent Compounds*?)

12. Uses of Diagrams to Test Validity of Schemata

If we have two predicates applying in our Universe, we may have things of four different kinds described by means of these predicates: for a given thing a in the universe there are four possibilities

1. a is F and a is G
2. a is F and a is G$'$
3. a is F$'$ and a is G
4. a is F$'$ and a is G$'$

So the object a may come in one of four different cells or compartments of the Universe.

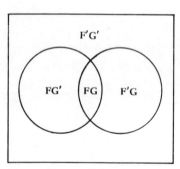

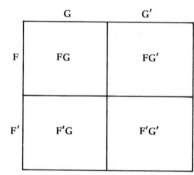

Venn diagram   Lewis Carroll diagram

The shape of the cells clearly doesn't matter logically, only the exhaustive division of the Universe into four cells. If we have three predicates we need *eight* cells:

56

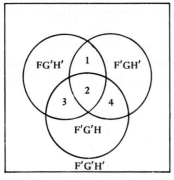

Venn Diagram

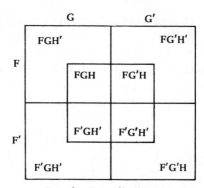

Lewis Carroll diagram

Cell 1 for FGH′; Cell 2 for FGH;
Cell 3 for FG′H; Cell 4 for F′GH′
For four predicates we need sixteen cells; and so on.

So far the diagrams tell us nothing about the Universe —
only shows us a logical possibility of classifying its contents.
To show categoricals in a diagram we put a mark in a cell to
show that it is emply (O) or non-empty (X). If we are given
premises and a conclusion:

1. If the premises and the contradictory of the conclusion
can be *together* represented in the diagram, this will be
because there is an interpretation that will make the premises
true and the conclusion false: so the form of argument is
invalid.

2. If the premises and the contradictory of the conclusion
cannot be together represented in the diagram, then this will
be because in representing the premises we have already
represented the conclusion and could not do otherwise: so
the form of argument will be *valid.*

The result will always go one way or the other, so this is a
decision procedure for the validity of categorical schemata.

It pays off if we represent emptiness of cells before trying to represent cells' being non-empty. If we must show e.g. that the FG cell is non-empty, we must represent this by putting X somewhere in the FG cell — but this doesn't tell us whether to put it in the FGH cell or the FGH′ cell. We could then use Lewis Carroll's dodge and put the X 'on the fence' between the two cells:

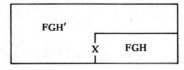

but we may not need to do this if the FGH cell is already marked as empty, since a X and a O cannot go into the same (undivided) cell: we then *must* mark the diagram thus:

Examples of valid and invalid schemata:

Every F is G; every F is H; *ergo* some G is H.
In existential form the premises are: FG′ = O, FH′ = O, and the *contradictory* of the conclusion is: GH = O. Let us see how to represent this information.

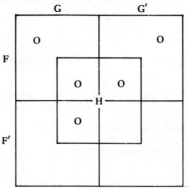

FG′ = O, so FG′H = O and FG′H′ = O. FH′ = O, so FGH′ = O and FG′H′ = O. GH = O, so FGH = O and F′GH = O. All this is represented in the diagram, so the argument is *invalid*. Notice, however, that if we adopted Lewis Carroll's way of reading 'every' proposition the premises would also give us the information: FG ≠ O, FH ≠ O. If we first represent FG′ = O, FH′ = O, we find we have to represent the further information as below:

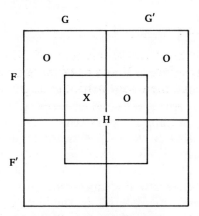

(After inserting the Os,
there is only one place
left to put the X within
the FG cell or the FH cell.)

We now *cannot* mark the GH cell as empty, so the argument is *valid*. This is no surprise, because the Lewis Carroll way of reading 'every' propositions makes them more informative, and a conclusion that doesn't validly follow when we have less information may follow when we have more. (Can a conclusion ever follow from more limited information, but be seen not to follow when we have further information?)

It is hard to draw four-term Venn diagrams (impossible with overlapping *circles*), but quite easy to draw four-term Lewis Carroll diagrams, thus:

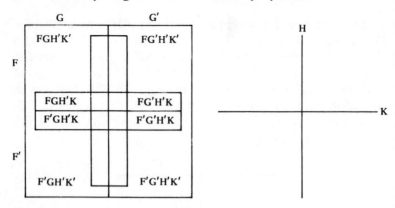

(i.e. the inside large vertical rectangle is the H cell, the inside large horizontal compartment is the K cell).

If we wish to represent a singular proposition of form '*a* is FG' say, then we simply use an asterisk instead of an X. Since an asterisk contains an X, this is meant to show that a cell containing an asterisk is marked as non-empty. The only extra rule we need is that since an individual cannot belong to two separate classes (e.g. *a* cannot be both FG and F′GH) we must put *only one* asterisk in the diagram if only one individual name figures in the premises — whereas there is no ban on inserting several Xs in the diagram.

EXERCISES

1. Label the squares left blank in the four-term diagram.

2. Interpreting the predicate-letters 'F,G,H' in a Universe of persons, show that this inference has a valid form:

    Every honest miller has a golden thumb
    No miller has a golden thumb
Ergo No miller is honest.

13. Plurative Propositions: Use of Diagrams for Plurative Schemata

We can use diagrams to test the validity of arguments using 'most' or 'half' as well as 'every', 'some', and 'no'. 'Most Fs are Gs' is to mean:

More objects in the Universe are FG than are FG$'$

'Half the Fs are Gs' is to mean:

At least as many objects in the Universe are FG as are FG$'$.

Propositions using the quantifiers 'most' and 'half' are called *plurative*.

There is a *decision method* for schemata containing categoricals of the ordinary sorts and also plurative propositions. We insert in each cell of a diagram a letter signifying the number of individuals of the Universe that are assigned to that cell. Then we construct from our data a set of propositions about the sums formed from these numbers and about whether one sum is or is not greater than another. As before:

If we can represent consistently the premises *and* the contradictory of the conclusion, we have an invalid schema.

If we cannot do this we have a valid schema.

Examples:

1. Most Fs are Gs; every G is H; *ergo* most Fs are H.

   Test for consistency:

There are more FGs than FG's, so	$a + c > b + d$ (1)
Every G is H,	so $a + g = 0$,
	so $a = 0, g = 0$ (2)

Not (most Fs are H), i.e. there
are *not* more FHs than FH's   so $c + d \not> a + b$ (3)

But now we have: $c > b + d$, and ⎫

from (1) and (2)   thus $c > b$ ⎬ contra-

from (2) and (3) $c + d \not> b$, and ⎨ diction

       thus $c \not> b$ ⎭

So the schema is valid.

2. Most Fs are Gs; most Gs are H; *ergo* some F is H.

   Test for consistency:

There are more FGs than FGs,	so $a + c > b + d$ (1)
There are more GHs than GHs,	so $c + e > a + g$ (2)
No F is H	so $c + d = 0, c = 0$,
	$d = 0$ (3)

We now have:

from (1) and (3) $a > b$

from (2) and (3) $e > a + g$

Obviously we can find numbers a,b,e,g, to fulfil these conditions: e.g. $a = 2, b = 1, g = 1, e = 4$. So the schema is invalid.

3. Most Fs are G; most Gs are H; most Hs are F; *ergo* some F is GH.

Test for consistency:

There are more FGs than FG's,	so $a + c > b + d$	(1)
There are more GHs than GH's,	so $c + e > a + g$	(2)
There are more HFs than HF's,	so $c + d > c + f$	(3)
There are *no* FGHs	so $c = 0$	(4)

By (1) and (4) $a > b + d$, so $a > d$

By (2) and (4) $e > a + g$, so $e > a$

By (3) and (4) $d > e + f$, so $d > e$

So we get $a > d$, $d > e$, $e > a$ — a contradiction. So the argument is valid.

EXERCISES

1. The premises of the argument about Swedes in Exercise 2, Chapter 7, may be represented by the following schema (with a Universe of people):

Most Fs are G; most FHs are G'

Show that the conclusion 'Most Fs are H'' does not follow but the conclusion 'Most FH's are G' does follow. Given your key of interpretation for the letters, how should this conclusion be read?

2. Using a four-term diagram, show that the following schema is valid:

Every F is G: most Gs are K: every K is H: most Hs are F
Ergo: some F is K.

3. From a report by the Rev. Jeremiah Prodnose on the morals of students at the University of Shrewsbury:

The bad habits of smoking, drinking, and obscenity are all prevalent; moreover, most smokers drink, most drinkers use obscene language, and most users of obscene language smoke. Some students indeed have all three bad habits; but these, happily, are comparatively few — fewer in fact than the class who only smoke but neither drink nor use obscene language, and fewer than the class who only drink and neither smoke nor use obscene language, and likewise fewer than the class who only use obscene language and neither smoke nor drink.

Are these statements logically consistent?

14. Turning Sound Arguments into New Arguments (Themata)

In the last two chapters we have been concerned with patterns of argument, sound and unsound. We shall now be concerned with methods for turning kinds of sound argument we already have into new sound arguments. The Stoic logicians called such a rule or method a *thema* — plural *themata*. This is a short word you can use if you wish: do not confuse *themata*, which are methods for forming *arguments* out of *arguments*, with argument *schemata*, which are patterns for inferring *propositions* from *propositions*. The starting-points and results are different. An argument, whose pattern is an argument-schema, starts from premises and ends with a conclusion. Any premise or conclusion is itself not an argument but a proposition — whether an asserted proposition or one just assumed for the space of the argument. No proposition is ever itself an argument; so a procedure for passing from one or more arguments known to be sound to the formulation of another sound argument is not *itself* an argument from premises to conclusion. That's why it is best to have a special name for such procedures.

(1) The simplest sort of thema is the chainlike ordering of arguments: whatever follows from a conclusion follows from its premises. If we have a sound argument from A and B to C, and another from C and D to E, and another from E to F, then we have a sound argument from A, B, and D to F.

A   B

C   D

E

F

As I said before, a physical chain may break either because it has a weak link or because it is too long: a logical chain can break only for the first reason — if (but only if) each link is sound, the whole chain is sound.

(2) The synthetic rule (discovered by pupils of Aristotle). This is an elaboration of the chain rule. Any conclusion drawn from our original stock of premises may be added to our premises to get new conclusions, and this increase in our stock may be repeated *ad lib*: all the conclusions thus reached are counted as conclusions from the *first* stock of premises. E.g. we may get D from A and B, then E from A and D, then F from B and D, then G from A, E and F; D, E, F, and G *all* follow from A and B; so we need no longer have the neat tree-like pattern of Rule (1).

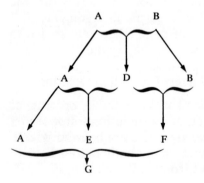

Notice that we repeat (or reiterate, as the technical term is) the use of A and B as premises; the arrows from A to A, or B to B, are all right, because obviously any proposition follows from itself.

The working of the synthetic rule depends on the fact that no addition to a stock of premises can stop a conclusion from following: whatever follows from B and C follows still if we add a new premise D.

The synthetic rule may not always have seemed obviously sound: in an obscure passage of the *Phaedo* Plato complains of 'enemies of reason who confuse together a first principle and the things derived from it'. Anyhow, in fact the question whether A follows from B and C does not in any way depend on how we got our B and C, nor on whether these are 'first principles' or not, nor on what other information we have besides B and C.

(3) Rules (1) and (2) only tell us how to fit arguments together to make a longer one: the other rules we are to study tell us how to get arguments with *different* premises and/or conclusions from arguments we already have.

Rule (3) is the rule for using *reductio ad absurdum*, which we've already looked at in Ch. 6 (Uses of argument). If premises, P,Q,R, . . . lead together to a contradiction, we do not (if we are sensible) conclude that we have *proved* a contradiction — rather, that there is something wrong with the premises. So if we retain Q,R, . . . we may derive from these the negation or contradictory of the remaining premise P. We have had such a move already in Chapter 13. Since the premises:

Most As are Bs; most Bc are Cs; most Cs are As; no A is BC together yield a contradiction, it follows that from the premises:

Most As are Bs; most Bs are Cs; most Cs are As we can infer the contradictory opposite of the remaining premise 'No A is BC', namely:

Some A is BC.

In general, logic does not tell us *which* premises we are to keep and infer that the remaining one must be rejected. (If the boat is sinking, *someone* may have to go overboard, but logic need not tell us *who*.)

(3A) From this rule we may derive a rule of *contraposition* which is often useful. If from A and B we could infer C, then from A and the negation of C we can infer the negation of B. For if C follows from A and B, then this set of premises:

A, the negation of C, B

leads to a contradiction — the negation of C (in the set already) *plus* C (derivable from A and B). So if we keep A and the negation of C as premises, we must reject B and infer the negation of B.

(4) A rule that looks almost too obvious to mention: Suppose that if we had premises A,B,C . . . we could infer conclusion P. Now suppose that we lack one of these premises, say B and that P *doesn't* follow from A,C, . . . All the same, we know that *something* follows from A,C, . . . just as they are: namely, the conditional formed with B and P — we know that from A,C, . . . it follows that *if* B is true then P is.

Example: From the premises:

All books on that shelf are blue; there's a copy of Caesar among the books on that shelf

we obviously get the conclusion 'There's a blue copy of Caesar on that shelf'

(It's obvious; but, for practice, work out a proof of this with the diagrams.)

From this we learn that from the *single* premise 'All the books on that shelf are blue' we can infer the conclusion:

If there's a copy of Caesar among the books on that shelf, *then* there's a blue copy of Caesar among the books on that shelf.

From this it is clear that the argument you get by applying rule (4) — called by logicians the *conditionalizing* rule — is different from the argument you started with. In the example, the original argument has *two* premises, and the conclusion is that *there is* a blue copy of Caesar on the shelf: the argument got by the conditionalizing rule — which must be sound if the argument we started with was sound (as it was indeed) — has *one* premise; and there is an 'if' in the conclusion, unlike the original conclusion.

(5) Dilemma. This is one of the few technical terms of logic that come up in ordinary language in a sense roughly corresponding to their logical meaning. It shows a way of plaiting together two arguments that reach the same conclusion along two different routes.

Suppose we have the conclusion P following by a sound argument from A,B,C, ... and also from D,E,F, ... Now suppose we're *not* given A as a premise, and *not* given D as a premise either, but *are* given as a premise that *either* A holds or D does. Then from *this* information together with the remaining premises — B,C, ... *plus* E,F, ... — we can infer the conclusion P. On one alternative, P follows from A,B,C, ... and on the other from D,E,F, ... ; so *anyhow* it follows from B,C, ... *plus* E,F, ... *plus* the 'either/or' premise.

Example:

P. Either B will drink the water in his water-bottle or he will not.

Alternative (i)	*Alternative* (ii)
Q. B will drink the water in his water-bottle.	V. B will not drink the water in his water-bottle.
R. The water in B's water-bottle is saturated with salt, and B is severely dehydrated	W. If B does not drink the water in his water-bottle B will get no water in the desert.
S. Anybody who drinks water saturated with salt and is severely dehydrated dies of thirst.	X. If B gets no water in the desert, B will die of thirst.
Therefore	Therefore
T. Bill will die of thirst.	T. Bill will die of thirst.

By Alternative (i) we have T following from Q,R, and S; by

Alternative (ii) we have T following from V,W, and X. Since P (which says that *either* Q *or* V is true) is obvious anyhow, we have T following from the set of premises R,S,W, and X — even if we don't know *which one* of the premises Q,V, is true.

DISCUSSION TOPICS

1. Go back over the difference (Ch. 4) between a statement and an argument, so as to be clear why themata, deriving *arguments* from *arguments*, are not a kind of argument.

2. Can arguments entwined as in the diagram for thema (2) go in a circle — could we complete the circle by arrows showing A and B derived from F and G? If not, why not? What is wrong with arguing in a circle?

3. Logic doesn't tell us *which* premises of an inconsistent set to drop: does this show a fault in logic? Could the fault be mended? If logic doesn't tell us, what does?

4. In my example of a dilemma the premise with an 'or' in it was obvious and 'goes without saying': construct a dilemma (i.e. an argument formed by the dilemma rule) where the 'or' premise *isn't* obvious.

5. Suppose I argue
P. A man with 100,001 hairs is not bald
Q. A man with one less hair than a man who isn't bald, isn't bald
R. *Ergo*, a man with 100,000 hairs isn't bald.
This seems all right — but now if I repeat this use of premise Q 100,000 times I get the conclusion that a man with no hair at all isn't bald! Does this not show that there *is* something like a chain's breaking because it's too long — even in logic?

15. Self-evidence, Logical Truth, and Analytic Propositions

Many propositions are evident but not self-evident. It is evident that there are many dogs around and that many men wear shoes: but so far as the meaning of the terms goes, dogs might be as extinct as dodoes and shoes as much out of fashion as togas. What is wrong with denying either of these propositions is that it is contrary to observations anybody can make. But we need no observation to show that either it is raining or it isn't, nor to show that 3 is odd. Propositions like these, evident independently of observation (or testimony or memory, for that matter), are called *self*-evident.

Not all propositions that can be shown true or false by mere logic are true or false self-evidently. The logical falsity of the proposition:

Some male barber living in Alcalá shaves all and only those males living in Alcalá who do not shave themselves

is nowise self-evident. (In fact some people have scented a logical antinomy here not resoluble by logic — since they assume there *could* be such a barber. Let his name be 'Juan': then does Juan shave himself or does he not? Either way, we get a contradiction! But what logic shows is that there can be no such barber; so not to worry — there is no basis for saying: Let *his* name be 'Juan'.) However, *all* truths of logic either are themselves self-evident or follow by evident methods of proof from self-evident truths of logic; and *ipso*

71

facto their contradictories are shown to be false.

It is wrong to suppose that only abstract logical or mathematical truths can be reached as logical conclusions; or that propositions about actual existence cannot be logically derived. It is just a matter of what your premises are; and premises relating to what actually exists, though not self-evident, may be evident and undeniable, like my examples about dogs and shoes.

Logical truths are tied up in a special way with valid forms of inference. Suppose we pick our readings of the letters 'p,q,r' (as propositions) in such a way that 'p,q, therefore r' is a logically valid inference. Then by the conditionalizing thema (see Chapter 13), 'p, therefore if q then r' will also represent a valid inference. If we now conditionalize once more, 'If p, then if q, then r' is true with *no* premises needed to prove it: true by logic. But this, which is a logically true proposition, must be carefully distinguished from the inference 'p, q, therefore r'.

Similarly, the point of 'Either p or not p' is that we can use it as a premise for argument shown to be valid by the dilemma rule (Chapter 14). We *can* use a meatier alternative than this for our 'Either . . . or . . .' premise, and this sort of premise really adds nothing to our information (like Belloc's 'He will buy you the creature or else he will not'). If someone begins by enunciating *this* premise with pomp and circumstance, look out! It may be like a conjuror making a pass to distract attention, for of course he has done nothing so far except to show he means to use a dilemma. Dilemmas are in fact often fallacious in concrete examples — not because the dilemma rule for constructing arguments is at all dubious, but because in practice it is often used to plait together unsound arguments, and so the result is unsound.

Mathematical truths are often not self-evident, e.g. Euclid's discovery that for any prime number there is a bigger one. The proof of that would never be found by brooding on what we really mean by 'prime number' and 'bigger' — Euclid had to think of a special trick for proving it. Finding new methods of proof has been the way mathematics has progressed. Gödel has proved that this is not just a matter of human ignorance: given *any* definitely specified methods of proof, there will *necessarily* be mathematical truths that cannot be proved just by using *those* methods — but only by adding new methods. In logic it is otherwise: the logical ideal is to find a repertoire of methods of proof that will encompass *all* the logical truths that can be expressed in a certain vocabulary — and for large areas of logic we know that this ideal can in fact be realized.

Statements outside logic and mathematics are often described as 'true in virtue of what the words mean'. But of course the most crassly factual statements are true or false in virtue of what the words mean: e.g. 'The pedestrian was on the pavement when the car hit him' may be true or false according as 'pavement' bears its U.S. or British sense. No doubt what people are after in using this description is: true *solely* in virtue of what the words mean. But it's doubtful whether this notion (often the term 'analytic proposition' is used to express it) is much use.

Both of these propositions — or rather, each separately — would be a good candidate for a proposition true solely in virtue of what the words mean:

A. All fathers are male.

B. Once a father, always a father: if X ever is Y's father, X remains Y's father so long as they both live. (Quine calls this the thesis of sempaternity.)

But from A and B it follows that no male that is a father can stop being male during the life of its offspring: and that isn't even true, let alone true by virtue of what the words mean. You could modify A or B; or you could say that the term 'father' doesn't mean quite the same in them both, although each of them is true in virtue of what the term means *there*. But if you do any of these things, you have to admit that intuitions about what is true in virtue of the meaning of words are pretty unreliable: that will certainly be so if 'father' in A has a different meaning from 'father' in B — how can you see the truth is determined by meaning when you are not sure just what the meaning of terms is?

DISCUSSION TOPICS

1. Are these propositions self-evident? Are they true because of what words mean?
    Nothing can be red and green all over
    Any figure of constant diameter is circular
    If three rings are interlaced so that they will not pull apart, them some two of them must be thus interlaced.

2. What makes a word a logical word? Try constructing a list. Consider which of the following are logical words:
    if, or, possibly, when, where, than, because, unless, until, certain, believe, word.
(Consult Quine and Ullian, Chapter III).

16. Propositional Logic: Truth-Functions

A proposition — a piece of informative language propounded for consideration — need not be always used to make a statement. As we saw in Chapter 6, there are other uses of argument than inference from *asserted* premises to an *asserted* conclusion, and a proposition may figure as premise or conclusion in such argument. It is equally important that a proposition may figure as a part of a longer proposition, and will still have a truth-value when it does so figure. For example: 'the Earth is flat' is false; this proposition is still false when it occurs as part of (1) and (2):

(1) It is not the case that the Earth is flat
(2) Jones believes that the Earth is flat

and it is just because it *is* false that we are warranted in regarding (1) as true and in inferring from (2) that Jones believes something that is not so.

The same form of words may on different occasions be used to propound now a true proposition, now a false one. Even on a single occasion one may be using an ambiguous form of words, or the audience may hear what is uttered as being said in different languages or dialects. What is required for the successful application of logic is not that we should adopt some linguistic conventions making ambiguity *impossible*, but simply that ambiguity is *in fact* excluded in the piece of argumentation we are presently conducting. As

Quine has said in *Methods of Logic* (New York, 3rd ed. 1972, pp. 48-9):

> Insofar as the interpretation of ambiguous expressions depends on circumstances of the argument as a whole — speaker, hearer, scene, date, and underlying problem and purpose — the fallacy of equivocation is not to be feared; for, those background circumstances may be expected to influence the interpretation of an ambiguous expression uniformly wherever the expression recurs in the course of the argument. This is why words of ambiguous reference such as 'I', 'you', 'here', 'Smith', and 'Elm Street' are ordinarily allowable in logical arguments without qualification; their interpretation is indifferent to the logical soundness of an argument, provided merely that it stays the same throughout the space of the argument.

In ordinary grammar we are familiar with the idea of a conjunction that joins two clauses to form a sentence. (Logicians prefer the word 'connective', because 'conjunction' is needed as a technical term.) The primary-school explanation, that a conjunction is any single word that will make good sense in between two sentences (e.g. 'but', 'although', 'before', 'after', etc. in the context

I ran to the station . . . the train was gone)

is good enough to start with. But we cannot always regard a sentence formed out of sub-clauses as a proposition formed out of two propositions. E.g.

(3) A married man must work or his family will suffer

The first half of (3), before the 'or', looks like a proposition all right. But we cannot treat 'his family will suffer' as a proposition, because there's no sense in trying to find its truth-value. Whether it is true or false that they will suffer depends on *who are* the people signified by 'his family' — but of course no particular family is being thought of, so there's no question whether 'they' really will suffer or not. Again, consider

(4) If a piece of iron is heated it expands

Is it true or false that a piece of iron is heated? Or again: that this piece of iron expands? (*Which* piece?!) We cannot regard this as having the structure 'If p then q', where the letters represent propositions with truth-values: the real structure is:

Any piece of iron/ expands when heated.

On the other hand there are plenty of examples where we *can* represent a proposition in a schema with schematic (propositional) letters for its sub-clauses. E.g.

(5) Socrates was wise and virtuous or Plato was an awful liar.

Schema '(p and q) or r': key of interpretation

p = Socrates was wise, q = Socrates was virtuous, r = Plato was an awful liar. Notice the importance of bracketing: 'p and (q or r)' would come out as:

(6) Socrates was wise; and he was virtuous too, or else Plato was an awful liar.

Notice also that if propositions are thus compounded, the compound is itself able to be compounded with other propositions to make more complex propositions.

Propositions identifiable as clauses of longer propositions may or may not be such that their truth-values fix the truth-values of the longer propositions. In a minor work, Lewis Carroll has a professor who makes a great collection of pairs of slips pinned together, with such entries as:

(7) The Head Cook recovered from fever.

(8) The Head Cook took a double dose of fever mixture.

If we abbreviate (7) to 'p' and (8) to 'q', then even if both are true this doesn't fix the truth-value of 'p because q', or of 'q and then p'. But 'It is the case both that p and that q' *must* be true if both 'p' and 'q' are true, and *must* be false if either or both should be false.

Like many things in logic, this was not always obvious. Aristotle at one time — not always — thought it was a logical error to demand a plain 'Yes or No' answer to a question 'Is it the case both that p and that q?', because neither answer would be suitable if e.g. 'p' were true and 'q' false. Bad logic books of today sometimes repeat Aristotle's mistake, and call the supposed logical error the Fallacy of Many Questions. (If you find this 'fallacy' — or the 'fallacy' of *ad hominem* argument, see Chapter 6 — given *as* a fallacy in a logic textbook, then don't buy the book!) Such a double question need not embarrass us at all. If you think 'p' is true and 'q' is false, then the answer you give to 'Is it the case that both p and q? Yes or no?' should be a plain No. And if the other fellow tries to make you admit that you've denied 'p', then he is just being sophistical.

We speak of the way of compounding propositions that we get in 'It is the case both that p and that q' as *truth-functional.* We apply the same term to 'It is not the case that . . .', because the result of applying this phrase to a proposition is true/false if the original proposition is false/true.

As we saw, 'it is not the case that p' is called the negation or *contradictory* of the proposition written as 'p'. We can often get an equivalent by inserting 'not' somewhere into the proposition to be negated; but this is not a mechanical or foolproof procedure; e.g. 'Some men are not wise' will not do duty for 'It is not the case that some men are wise'.

'(It is the case that both) p and q (and r . . .)' is called the *conjunction* of the propositions abbreviated to 'p','q',('r' . . .), and these propositions are called *conjuncts* of the conjunction.

The term 'truth-function', from which 'truth-functional' derives, is a generalization by Frege from the ordinary mathematical use of 'function'. Given an ordinary mathematical function, say the square function or the cube function, we can construct a table showing what the *value* of the function is for different *arguments*. (The last word is a technical term, simply to be learned: nothing to do with 'argument' in the familiar sense we have used up to now.)

E.g.   when the argument x   is 0, 1, 2, 3, 4
       the value of x^2 is 0, 1, 4, 9, 16
       and the value of x^3 is 0, 1, 8, 27, 64

Obviously tables cannot give the values of a numerical function for *all* arguments. But there are only two truth-values – truth (T) and falsehood (F). So for a pair of propositions we get only four possible assignments of truth-values:

p	T	F	T	F
q	T	T	F	F

If we now have a proposition formed out of 'p' and 'q' whose truth-value is fixed given merely the truth-values of 'p' and 'q', we call this proposition a *truth-functional* compound of 'p' and 'q'. For example, conjunction is a truth-functional compound, because we can make a complete table of the truth-values for 'p ∧ q' (short for 'It is the case both that p and that q') showing how they are determined by the truth-values of 'p' and 'q':

p	T	F	T	F
q	T	T	F	F
p ∧ q	T	F	F	F

Negation is a truth-functional compound of the proposition negated: we have this truth-table for negation (where the prefix means 'it is not the case that . . .?'):

p	T	F
¬p	F	T

Another important truth-functional way of compounding propositions is *disjunction*. Here there is a minor trouble about how to fill one place in the truth-table:

p	T	F	T	F
q	T	T	F	F
p or q	?	T	T	F

It is not always clear whether a proposition of the form 'p or q' is meant to exclude, or not to exclude, the case where both are true. (It is just silly to discuss which sense of 'or' is *right*: not too silly for some people to discuss it.) We can remove this ambiguity in English by saying 'p or q, but not both' for the exclusive sense of 'or', and 'p or q or both' for the non-exclusive sense. Other languages can make the distinction less clumsily: Latin 'vel', Polish 'lub', are used mainly for 'or' in the non-exclusive sense, and Latin 'aut', Polish 'albo', for 'or' in the exclusive sense. In logical notation we write 'p ∨ q' for the non-exclusive 'or': truth-table:

p	T	F	T	F
q	T	T	F	F
p ∨ q	T	T	T	F

so that 'either p or q' ('p ∨ q') and 'neither p nor q' ('¬p ∧ ¬q') are contradictories. (Check this with truth-tables!) The exclusive 'or' can be expressed by:

$$(p \lor q) \land \neg (p \land q).$$

There is no standard shorthand for this: if we need one, we can write 'p *aut* q'.

Truth-functional consequences

Suppose we have an argument-schema satisfying the following conditions:

(i) The schema consists of *propositional* schematic letters which figure in the premise or premises and the conclusion of the schema either alone or in truth-functional compounds.

(ii) No reading of the letters will make the premises true and the conclusion false.

Then the conclusion is a *truth-functional consequence* of the premise(s), and *any* concrete argument got by interpreting the letters will be logically valid.

We can know *whether* condition (ii) is satisfied, given that we know *that* condition (i) is satisfied. For by the very meaning of 'truth-functional compound' we need not know anything except the *truth-values* of the propositions we use as readings for the letters in order to determine the truth-values of the premises and the conclusions in the schema; so we need only check the (finitely many) possible assignments of truth-values to the letters in order to see whether condition (ii) is fulfilled — whether there is *any* such assignment that makes the premises come out all with T and the conclusion with F. If not, the argument schema is valid.

N.B. It would be a gross error to suppose that an argument-schema which *does not* give a truth-functional consequence is invalid in all its instances — of course one that *does* give a truth-functional consequence is valid in all its instances. Any two-premise argument is an instance of the schema 'p,q, therefore r', and of course this doesn't give a truth-functional consequence because we can choose true propositions for 'p' and 'q' and a false one for 'r': but some arguments with two premises are valid.

Truth-functional tautologies
This term means: truth-functional schemata that *always* come out with the value T no matter what truth-values are assigned to the letters in them. A simple example is 'p ∨ ¬p'. If 'A' represents a premise (or the conjunction of the premises) of a truth-functional *argument* schema, and 'B' represents the conclusion, then if 'B' is a truth-functional consequence of 'A', '¬A ∨ B' and equivalently '¬(A ∧¬B)' will represent a truth-functional tautology: for by the definition 'truth-functional consequence', no reading of the letters in the formula abbreviated as 'A' and 'B' will make 'A' come out true and 'B' come out false, so '¬A ∨ B' and '¬(A ∧¬ B)' always come out true. 'E.g. 'p, q, *ergo* (p *aut* q) *aut* (p ∨ q)' is valid — the conclusion is a truth-functional consequence of the premises — so '¬(p ∧ q) ∨ ((p *aut* q) *aut*

(p ∨ q))' is a truth-functional tautology. (Check that the schema given is a valid schema.)

Ordinary language varieties of truth-functional compounds
Conjunction may be represented by 'and' pure and simple, or again by 'but' or 'although': the use of 'but' or 'although' before a clause 'does not *change* the sense of the clause but only *throws light* on it in a peculiar way' (Frege). – N.B.: clauses joined by any of these connectives, even the plain 'and', may not be propositions with assignable truth-values and may not be forming a truth-functional compound.

Disjunction may be represented by 'unless' rather than 'or':

You will get that cannon in position or half of you will be shot.

Unless you get that cannon in position, half of you will be shot.

EXERCISES

1. Verify by truth-tables that 'p ∧ q' is the contradictory of '⅂p ∨ (p ∧⅂q)' i.e. that '⅂ (p ∧ q)' is a truth-functional consequence of '⅂p ∨ (p ∧⅂q)' and conversely '⅂ (⅂p ∨ (p ∧⅂q))' is a truth-functional consequence of 'p ∧ q'.

2. Consider the key of interpretation:
p = Socrates once kicked a dog   q = the dog bit Socrates
Are 'p ∧ q' and '⅂p ∨ (p ∧⅂q)' contradictories with this key of interpretation? If not, why not?

3. Can the following proposition be put in the form 'p ∧ q'? If so, how should the letters be read?
A plumber called this morning and his mate went back for some tools.

4. Can the following proposition be put in the form 'p v q' or 'p *aut* q'?

No stranger can have come in the night, or the dog would have barked. (Assume a suitable context of utterance, so that we know which night and which dog is in question.)

5. Are 'p ∧ q' and 'q ∧ p' truth-functional consequences of each other if we use the key of interpretation: p = Tom and Mary got married, q = Tom and Mary had a baby? If not, why not?

Can 'Tom and Mary got married' be put in the form 'p ∧ q'?

17. Explanation

In the present context 'explanation' will mean, not simply any procedure for making things plain or clear, but an answering of the question 'Why?' (Similarly, 'hypothesis' will mean, not just any proposition assumed as a premise without being asserted, but one so assumed with a view to finding reasons why.)

The question 'Why?' may mean 'Why do we/you affirm that?' or 'Why is that so?' We are here concerned only with the second use of 'Why?'

This question is not always reasonable. As regards a mathematical assertion, for example, there is no sense in asking why it is true − one can only ask how it is known to be true. 'Why?' sometimes relates to what the medievals called efficient causes (causes that bring things about) and sometimes to what they called final causes (the ends or goals for which things happen); but it was rightly said in medieval times that neither sort of explanation has a place in mathematics. (Nothing does happen in mathematics: the dramatic language of geometry − cutting, dropping, etc. − is merely a spur to pupils' jaded attention.)

Again, upon the whole we do not ask for explanations of negative facts. An hotel guest might ask 'Why is there no soap?' but hardly 'Why are there no snakes?' − one expects soap, but not snakes. Very often the suitable reply to 'Why no A?' is 'Why *should* there be an A?' − But what role do 'why' and 'should' play in this rejoinder?

There is a Jewish story that it is fruitful to meditate upon in this connexion. Two Rabbinical scholars were reading the Law. They had not got very far − in fact not beyond *Genesis*

1,1, which contains the word 'eretz' ('earth'). The initial question of the dialogue which follows is just like asking in English: Why should there be a letter G in the word 'earth'? — *gimel* being the corresponding letter in Hebrew.

> Why should there be a *gimel* in 'eretz'?
> But there isn't a *gimel* in 'eretz'!
> Then why isn't there a *gimel* in 'eretz'?
> Why should there be a *gimel* in 'eretz'?
> Well, that's what I just asked you!

Again, coincidences of events in general call for no explanation; if the separate events are explained, that may be that. There may be a reason why one evening Jung was writing up his case history of a patient who had a thing about beetles, and also a reason why that evening a beetle was bumbling around near Jung: there need be no reason for what Jung calls synchrony — for both happening together — and to look for *further* reasons-why is a typically superstitious attitude.

There are various types of explanation: and people have different dispositions to accept one or another type.

(i) Because given what had previously happened it was *necessary* that this should happen.

(ii) Because this is what *always or regularly* happens.

(iii) Because someone (God or man) simply so *chose.*

(iv) Because that is *the best way* for things to have happened.

The chief difficulty about type (i) explanations is that causal following differs in this way from logical following: If A logically follows from B and C, A logically follows from B and C and D; but if A causally follows from the factors B and C, the presence of a further factor D may prevent A from following.

Type (iv) is a barren sort of explanation. One could hardly calculate the answer to the question 'How much water is there in the sea?' by starting from 'There's just as much as there ought to be'. Leibniz said God created this world because it was the best possible world; but surely 'best possible world' is a self-contradictory description like 'crookedest possible line'?

Part of the philosophical trouble about free choice is whether we are to accept type (ii) or type (iii) explanations. The Tsar of Russia was not satisfied with the explanation that there was a soldier on guard in a grass plot because there *always* was — standing orders!; he worked back to the will of Empress Catherine that a guard should protect a snowdrop, i.e. back from type (ii) to type (iii) explanation. One might say of course that there are some rules of what *always* happens that would explain Catherine's imperial caprice — though in fact no such rules are actually statable. Similarly the Continuous Creation theory is preferred by some to the Big Bang theory because hydrogen would trickle into being in a *regular* way — as opposed to one unique event long ago. (Cf. Wittgenstein's *Tractatus* 6.732:

> Thus people today stop at the laws of nature, treating them as something inviolable, just as God and Fate were treated in past ages.

> And in fact both are right and both wrong: though the view of the ancients is clearer in so far as they have a clear and acknowledged terminus, while the modern system tries to make it look as if *everything* were explained.)

A further type of explanation, whose import and relation to other types are much disputed, is *teleological* explanation; answering a question 'Why?' with 'In order that so-and-so'. ('Why have veins got valves? In order that the blood may flow along them only towards the heart.') Answers of this type are of *heuristic* value in biology: J.Z. Young recently found out how the pineal body works by assuming it had some function. ('A happened in order that B should' is nowise in conflict with 'B happened because A had'.)

Explanation by 'what always happens' runs into the difficulty that there are all sorts of ways in which what happens recently and locally could be made to fit into a rule about what happens always and everywhere — these different projections being quite incompatible. Choosing what seems to us the simplest projection can hardly be anything more than a matter of our laziness. Nor will it do to say that our projections must be based on sound habits or else we wouldn't have survived. Think of Bertrand Russell's chicken: on the basis of past experience it runs to the farmer for corn every day; one day he wrings its neck — but meanwhile it has propagated its kind. The extent to which our projections of present experience *need* to be accurate in order that the human race should have survived is far smaller than the light-years of space and millions of years of time over which in science we *do* make projections; and advanced science may have a negative survival value, one way or another, by pollution or by war.

Nor is it true that we men simply cannot help having those habits of forming hypotheses, about what happens always and everywhere, that we do have: a culture can exist and flourish that has radically different habits. The Aztecs, so Prescott tells us, believed that every fifty-two years there was a cosmic crisis, after which the course of nature might change: so they locked up all the pregnant women (because monsters might now be born) and put out all the fires — and at midnight of the end of the cycle tried to light a fire. If it lit, the course of nature was set for another fifty-two years as before. It was too bad that soon after one new cycle had begun the Spaniards came, with horses and iron and gunpowder that had never been known before... But, as I said, our habits of forming scientific hypotheses may bring us to disaster too.

DISCUSSION TOPICS

1. Can survival value be used (a) to explain the fact that organs of living things appear to subserve ends? (b) to justify some human habit of belief or practice? How far can it be thus used?

2. Can one form of explanation be reduced to another? Is one superior or prior to another?

   (Read Socrates in Plato's *Phaedo* on different ways of explaining why he sits still in prison.)

18. Hypotheticals

Roughly speaking, hypotheticals are sentences joined together with an 'if'. We don't count, however, sentences like 'I paid you back that fiver, if you remember', 'There's whisky in the decanter if you want a drink'; for here the speaker is committed to asserting outright — not *if* something else is so — 'I paid you back that fiver' or 'There's whisky in the decanter'. Nor do we count sentences where 'if' means 'whether': 'I doubt if he'll come' (quite good English, whatever nagging schoolmasters say). Nor do we count cases where 'if' has to be paraphrased with 'and':

If you say that, he may hit you = Possibly (you'll say that *and* he'll hit you)
If it rains it sometimes thunders = Sometimes (it rains *and* it thunders).

Even with these odd cases excluded, not every hypothetical can be put in the form 'If p then q', because the clauses of the hypothetical may have no truth-value (even if we assume a given context of utterance). 'If you tease a camel, it spits at you' is an example: it would be irrelevant to ask 'Is it true or false that you tease a camel? and does it or does it not spit at you?' We may distinguish between *general hypotheticals* and *hypotheticals proper*: the logical form of the 'camel' sentence is better shown thus (to allow for the general force of 'you': interpreting 'you' like French 'on', or German 'man'):

As regards *any* man and *any* camel: if he teases it, then it spits at him.

The view has been held that a man who asserts an 'If p then q' hypothetical is not really asserting anything unless 'p' is true, and that if 'p' is true he is saying something true/false according as 'q' is true/false. This is all right as regard bets: 'If Bonnyboy wins today, then I bet £5 that he'll win tomorrow'. The £5 is safe unless Bonnyboy wins today: and the bet is then won/lost according as Bonnyboy wins/loses the next day. But consider the form of inference (called *modus tollens*) 'If p, then q: but not q: *ergo* not p'. This is clearly valid; but on the view of hypotheticals we are discussing it couldn't be valid, for by drawing the conclusion 'not p' we'd be making the assertion of the premise 'If p then q' into a nullity.

There are technical terms for two other valid moods and two fallacies:

Modus ponens: If p, then q: but p: *ergo* q.
Hypothetical syllogism: If p, then q; if q, then r; *ergo*, if p, then r.
Fallacy of affirming the consequent: If p, then q; but q; *ergo* p?!
Fallacy of denying the antecedent: If p, then q; but not p; *ergo* not q?!

If we admit the validity of *modus ponens* and *reductio ad absurdum*, we can show that from 'If p then q' there follows '¬(p ∧ ¬q)'. For suppose we have the premises (1) 'If p then q' and (2) 'p ∧ ¬q'. From (2) there follows (3) 'p', and from (3) and (1) by *modus ponens* (4) 'q'. But from (2) there also follows (5) '¬q'; (4) and (5) yield (6) 'q ∧ ¬q' — a flat contradiction. So if we keep premise (1), we may infer from it, by the *reductio ad absurdum* rule, the negation of premise (2), namely (7) '¬(p ∧ ¬q)'; which was to be proved.

If we admit the conditionalizing rule (Ch. 14) then we can show that conversely from '¬(p ∧ ¬q)' there follows 'If p then q'. For by truth-functional logic, from premises (1) '¬(p ∧ ¬q)' and (2) 'p' there follows (3) 'q'. So, by the conditionalizing rule, from the single premise (1) there follows a conditional with (2) as antecedent, (3) as consequent: namely (4) 'If p then q', which was to be proved.

Thus 'If p then q' and '¬(p ∧¬q)' come out logically equivalent. But this has paradoxical consequences.

(i) '¬(p ∧¬q)' is always true if 'p' is false. But we certainly do not count all hypotheticals with false antecedents as automatically true. In particular this is not true of what are called *contra-factual* or *subjunctive* conditionals — the latter name a schooldays' memory of translation into Latin. 'If Hitler had invaded in 1941 Hitler would have conquered England' doesn't count as true just because Hitler didn't invade in 1941. ('Subjunctive' is a better name than 'contra-factual'; for all hypotheticals of this class *would* have antecedent and consequent in the subjunctive mood in Latin — however useless this information is to people who know no Latin. — whereas it is *not* part of the truth-conditions that the antecedent should be false. 'If Bill had had any sense he'd have asked Mary to marry him' is not refuted, rather one's judgment is confirmed, if one is told that Bill *had* plenty of sense and *did* ask Mary to marry him.)

Subjunctive conditionals sometimes seem to offer a free play of fancy ('If Napoleon had been born a British subject. . .') and sometimes are logically beyond rational treatment ('If you were a bear you'd not like being baited'). And one gets such conflicting pairs as:

If Bizet and Verdi had had the same country, Bizet would have been Italian — Verdi would have been French.

But sometimes such clashes come in deadly earnest contexts; as in *R. v. Merrifield*:

Defence: If the deceased had not been given rat poison, she'd have died just as fast from liver disease.

Prosecution: If the deceased had not had liver disease, she'd have died just as fast from rat poison.

A lot sometimes hangs on which subjunctive conditional we go by; in this case, it was the prisoner that had to hang.

(ii) '¬(p ∧ ¬q)' is a truth-functional compound of 'p' and 'q' (cf. Ch. 16). We may verify by truth-tables that the following forms of inference are valid (writing 'p → q' for ¬(p ∧ ¬q)):

(a) (p ∧ q) → r; *ergo* (p → r) ∨ (q → r)

(b) (p → q) → r, ¬p, *ergo* r

(c) p → r, (p ∧ q) → ¬r, *ergo* p → ¬q.

But if we read 'p → q' as 'If p then q', there appear to be commonsense counter-examples to all three forms.

(a) p = Jim turns the key at 6.00, q = Bill turns the key at 6.00,

   r = The missile is fired just after 6.00.

(b) p = It's going to rain tomorrow, q = The Engineers won't play tomorrow, r = The Engineers are no good at football. (Imagine the Philosophers' football match coach using this case of (b) in a pep talk the day before they play the Engineers: he asserts the premise '¬p' because he believes the weather forecast. But in fact the Engineers win 6—1.)

(c) p = I flip the switch at 6.00, q = I remove the fuse at 5.59,

   r = The light goes on just after 6.00.

The right thing to say, I think, is that there is *a* use of 'if' for which the conditionalizing rule is valid, and for *this* use 'If p then q' may be written as '¬(p ∧ ¬q)' (or 'p → q', which *by definition* is the same thing); but that this isn't the *only* use of 'if' in ordinary-language conditionals. The modern dispute which use of 'if' is the *right* one is simply silly — like the old (and not quite dead) dispute about the right use of 'or': exclusive or nonexclusive?

EXERCISES

1. Which of the following are (a) general hypotheticals (b) hypotheticals proper (c) ambiguous as to which way one should take them?
    (i) If the Sun is in Aries it is spring in Europe.
    (ii) If a man is cheated he is wise afterwards.
    (iii) If Socrates was out late his wife nagged him.
    (iv) If Socrates was a bad man Plato was a liar.

2. Three men, Allen, Brown and Carr, keep a barber's shop. There is always one of them at work in shop hours. Allen, who has had fever (so his hand shakes), only goes out with Brown. Carr is the best at shaving. A logician, wishing to convince himself that when he calls he'll find Carr available, reasons as follows:
    (i) If Carr is out, then if Allen is out Brown is in.
    (ii) If Allen is out, Brown is *not* in.
    (iii) So, if Carr is out, (ii) is false. (Compare (ii) and the complex consequent of (i).)
    (iv) So Carr is *not* out — *modus tollens* from (iii) and (ii).
Is his reasoning sound?

DISCUSSION TOPIC

Customer.   I'll buy the car only if, if I buy the car, you'll guarantee it.
Salesman.   But let's suppose that if you buy the car, then I'll guarantee it: what then?
Customer.   Then I'll buy the car.
Salesman.   Can I hold you to both the things you've just said?

Customer.   Certainly.
Salesman.   Then you are logically committed to buying the car anyhow, even if I don't guarantee it.
Customer.   What?!
Salesman.   You say you'll buy the car only on condition that if you buy the car I'll guarantee it?
Customer.   Yes, I do say that: I'm not a complete idiot!
Salesman.   Well then: if you'll buy the car, you'll buy the car only if I'll guarantee it. Right?
Customer.   Uh-uh.
Salesman.   But in logic 'p only if q' is just a variant of 'if p then q'; so 'if p, then p only if q' is equivalent to 'if p, then if p then q' — and that's equivalent to 'if p, then q'.
Customer.   What on earth has that got to do with my buying the car?
Salesman.   You said that if you'll buy the car, then you'll buy the car only if I'll guarantee it. But that, you see, is logically equivalent to saying that if you'll buy the car then I'll guarantee it.
Customer.   Never mind what is logically equivalent to what! *Will* you guarantee the car?
Salesman.   I'm not saying anything about that just now. You said — remember? — that I can hold you to what *you*'ve said. And you've as good as said that if you'll buy the car then I'll guarantee it.
Customer.   Well, yes, it looks as if I did say that.
Salesman.   But you also said that, on condition that if you'll buy the car I'll guarantee it, you undertake you'll buy the car.
Customer.   Yes, I did.
Salesman.   But you are logically committed, as we just saw, to saying that the condition you stipulated is fulfilled: namely, that if you'll buy the car then I'll guarantee it.
Customer.   — * — ? * ! *

Salesman. So you've just got to buy the car, guarantee or no guarantee.

Customer. But I said that I'll buy the car only if you'll guarantee it. So if I am going to buy the car — as you pretend to have proved I must — you've got to guarantee it.

Salesman. I don't have to accept that. You said I could hold *you* to what *you* said: that's all I've been doing. *I'm* not bound by what *you* said, obviously. So it's a deal. I see you have your Access card there, Sir. Thank you very much, Sir. Please sign here.

(Due to Robert Hambourger)

19. Practical Reasoning

Theoretical reasoning is concerned with how things are; practical reasoning, with what is to be done.

Grammarians divide our discourse into some such classes as: statements, questions, commands, wishes, and exclamations. Logic hardly applies to wishes ('Would I had wings!') or exclamations ('How silly that was!'); and though work is in progress, there is no firm logical answer to the question 'What counts as an answer to a given question?' – a problem that examiners sometimes have to decide. But the matter is the less urgent, because so long as you stick to questions you cannot fall into inconsistency. (Incidentally, the answer to a question may be either a statement or a command.)

Commands, however, like statements, may form a covertly inconsistent set, which can be shown inconsistent only by logic. Since in both cases you can tolerate inconsistency only at the price of error or frustration, logic matters.

Grammar books apply 'command' or 'imperative' to other things besides the orders of superiors – prayers, entreaties, suggestions, etc. Logic can abstract from the differences. It is not even logically important that a second person should be involved; a shopping list has the same role in guiding a man's actions whether he drew it up himself or his wife did – and a different role from a list of the man's purchases made by a detective (which is a sort of propositional role). If there's a purchase on the list that has not been made, the shopper would typically put things right by making a new purchase – the detective, by scratching off an item from the list. We may speak perhaps of 'directives' or 'fiats' to avoid the wrong suggestion of 'commands', just as we've been speaking of 'propositions' rather than 'statements'.

Logic does not prescribe which practical premises we should accept, any more than it supplies premises for theoretical reasoning; for useful discussion we need agreement on premises. Allegedly such agreement is far harder to reach on practical matters of policy than on theoretical matters. But of course we do agree to an enormous extent in our own community about what is to be done, or our lives would be poor, nasty, brutish, and short; and in spite of recent events there is general international agreement on what is called 'the comity of nations', e.g. that the persons of ambassadors are immune from attack, or else all international relations would be war with no holds barred.

It is no good trying to discriminate between theoretical and practical discourse on this kind of ground. People say agreement can be reached on scientific but not moral matters; but the population whose opinion is polled is likely to be different in the two cases; and why should one worry more about the deviant moral views of New Guinea cannibals or Christian Scientists than about their deviant scientific views?

Let us suppose a man accepts a set of directives A,B,C, . . . formulating his ends and wishes to infer from these what he is to do. Let us also suppose that his ends are all consistently realizable in this hard world. Then the procedure of practical reasoning that suits this case may be described as follows: Suppose that D is a feasible directive whose fulfilment will guarantee the fulfilment of at least one of the directives originally accepted, A,B,C, . . . and will not be inconsistent with any of them. Then it is reasonable to add D to the set of directives we accept, and we repeat the procedure with the directives D,A,B,C, . . . And so on until we come to some directive X that can be immediately acted on.

Notice that though there is a parallel in this process to the synthetic rule for theoretical reasoning (see Ch. 14) there are several important differences.

(i) In theoretical reasoning it cannot be equally justifiable to pass from A,B,C, ... to a conclusion D and to an incompatible conclusion D'. But in practical deliberation D may be a fiat expressing one way of getting our ends, and D' may express another incompatible way: in that case it may be *up to us* whether from A,B,C, ... we pass on to accepting D as a guide to action, or rather, to accepting D'.

(ii) Imagine a conspirator who has to secure that Jones doesn't go to the meeting and a detective who has to trace Jones's movements. The conspirator reasons: 'Jones mustn't go to the meeting. If he misses the 5.30 he can't go to the meeting; making him miss the 5.30 wouldn't clash with our other plans: so Jones mustn't catch the 5.30'. The detective reasons: 'Jones didn't go to the meeting. If he missed the 5.30 he couldn't go to the meeting; assuming he missed the 5.30 wouldn't clash with our other information: so Jones must have missed the 5.30'. The conspirator's practical reasoning is sensible, the detective's theoretical reasoning is silly.

(iii) An added premise can never invalidate a piece of theoretical reasoning, but may invalidate a piece of practical reasoning: for if there is one more end to be secured, a fiat stating a policy that fits in with our other ends may not be reconcilable with this end.

This account of practical reasoning (indeed the verbal contrast between 'theory' and 'practice') comes in its essentials from Aristotle: 'principle' (from Latin 'principum', 'beginning') in moral discussions is a translation of Aristotle's 'archē', 'starting-point', and reflects (perhaps a little distortedly) his idea that we start from fiats stating the ends in view.

Among our starting-points will be facts that we *decide* to accept and not try to alter: 'don't run your head against a brick wall'. When a letter to a newspaper said 'General

Gland's argument is faulty because there is a missing premise: the existence of Communist China', the criticism would be sound if General Gland's argument were a piece of practical reasoning, and if the policy advocated by General Gland would be incompatible with his accepting in practice that Communist China will continue to exist. (Of course General Gland might reply that he saw it as no objection to a policy that it would require the destruction of Communist China.)

The model of practical reasoning that I've given does not show which end must be sacrificed, and how far, if we *cannot* fulfil all our ends. Nor does it show how to reconcile A and B in practical disagreement; but one useful consideration is that A and B may realise that some policy, e.g. avoiding atomic war, is a necessary condition of securing either A's ends or B's conflicting ends — and may accordingly agree on that policy.

DISCUSSION TOPICS

1. Some philosophers would say that I've only described prudential reasoning, not moral reasoning. Is there a difference in the style of reasoning, or rather in the choice of premises?

2. Is there a justification for counting heads differently in matters of science and in matters of morals? If so, what is it?

3. Construct a piece of practical reasoning and consider what added premises there could be to invalidate it.